DAUGHTER

A memoir

ISBN 978-1-970125-18-4

Daughter is a memoir. It reflects the author's present recollections of events in the past. Some scenes have been compressed or recreated, though their essence remains accurate. Some names and identifying characteristics have been changed to protect the privacy of persons concerned. Some of the dialogue in this book is verbatim, some is recreated to the best of the author's memory, and some is a mixture of both. While the stories in this book are true, the author recognises that others may have their own versions of the events described.

ALDA SIGMUNDSDÓTTIR

DAUGHTER

A memoir

For my daughter Aldís

PART I

The most beautiful word on the lips of mankind is the word 'Mother,' and the most beautiful call is the call of 'My mother.' It is a word full of hope and love, a sweet and kind word coming from the depths of the heart. The mother is everything – she is our consolation in sorrow, our hope in misery, and our strength in weakness. She is the source of love, mercy, sympathy, and forgiveness.

- Khalil Gibran

PROLOGUE

When I was a little girl my mother and I fought all the time, so she decided that I should see a psychiatrist. I was eight years old.

On the day of the appointment, she picked me up from the day-care centre where I went after school and together we walked to the child psychiatric ward of the National Hospital. It took us around twenty minutes. It was springtime, and buds were just forming on the trees and bushes that we passed. The sun was out, but the air was still cool, and I shivered in my light winter jacket. My mother strode along purposefully and I strove to keep up with her, not sure what this meeting was for, or why I needed to go.

In the waiting area were a handful of chairs, and a low table designed for children, with crayons and paper. I did not sit at the children's table but took a seat next to my mother, dangling my feet off the edge of the chair. A few minutes later a door opened and a tall man with a bulky physique and unruly hair stood in the doorway. He invited us into his office and introduced himself as Karl. He took a seat behind a big desk, my mother and I sat opposite, and after they had conversed for a bit he began asking me questions: What was my favourite subject in school; what did I like to do in my spare time; how did I get along with my mother; how did I feel about my father living apart from us? Eventually he pulled out a piece of cardboard that had been folded in two, and opened it. In the middle was a blob of something.

"Does this remind you of anything?" he asked, watching me closely.

I leaned over to examine it, then looked at him, puzzled. I wanted to give him the right answer, but was confused. He gave a genial smile. "Just tell me if you think this looks like anything."

It looked like a big blob of ink to me, but obediently I said: "It's kind of like an elephant."

He glanced at the blob and nodded thoughtfully.

"Very good," he said. "I'm going to talk to your mother now and was wondering if you would mind going out into the hall and drawing me a picture?"

"Of what?"

"Anything you want." He smiled benignly.

I went out and glanced back to see the door close behind me. I sat at the low kid's table and got to work.

By the time the door opened again my masterpiece was ready. I had drawn a house with a chimney and a garden, a flag pole with the Icelandic flag at full mast, a tree, and a winding path leading to the door. I handed the picture to the doctor, sincerely hoping he would like it.

"That's a good picture," he said, taking his seat behind the desk again. "I notice there are no people in it."

"I'm not good at drawing people," I said.

More questions ensued, then I was sent out into the hallway again for a few minutes while the doctor and my mother wrapped things up.

Later that evening I overheard my mother on the phone, telling her eldest sister Alma about the session. The doctor's verdict was that I was normal. Our fighting was also normal, and stemmed from the fact that we were too much alike, he said. If we ever *stopped fighting*, he told my mother, *that* was when she should bring me to see him.

There was a hint of triumph in her voice as she said it, as though this gave her some kind of one-upmanship. Which I would later learn was, indeed the case–my mother and Alma disagreed when it came to child-rearing methodology, and my mother was very keen to prove Alma wrong, and herself right.

I now know that Karl had no idea what he was looking at. *None.* Although how could he have been expected to see the threads that were woven in secret and kept resolutely hidden behind the façade of loving motherhood? Even I, who was the most immediate party to them, was unable to view the insidious tapestry they were weaving.

It was not until my half-sister Frances came to visit me, some four decades later, that I saw the evidence laid out before me, crystal-clear. Frances, who was nearly twenty years my junior, was sitting at my kitchen table wearing her Queen's University varsity jacket, while I was at the sink rinsing some dishes. I do not recall the exact topic we were discussing, only that she suddenly said: "I know why you didn't come to visit. I know it was because of my dad."

I had been standing with my back to her, and now spun around. Before I had a chance to comment she raised her left hand, made a sharp movement across it with the index finger of her right hand, and said emphatically: "If I could rid myself of his DNA by cutting my own wrists, *I would do it.*"

Her dark, almond-shaped eyes–our mother's eyes–burned with an acrimonious fire. I knew, right then, that I could not say what I was thinking: that her father was an easy man to hate, but that there was more–so much more. I could not say it because of her evident presumption that we were allies, that she and I were united with our mother against her father. That it was all about *him*, and in no way about *her.*

And then, with a creeping sense of dread, came the absolute inner knowing that where my mother had failed with me, she had succeeded with Frances.

MAR 1967

CHAPTER 1

As children, we gravitate towards light, because only in light can we grow. Like plants, we turn to the sun, for it is our birthright to flourish.

In one of my earliest memories, I am standing in front of a large window in the corridor of our apartment building in Reykjavík, looking down from the fifth floor onto the street below. The corridor is dark, and the scene framed by the window is like a painting–the sky a palette of rapidly fading golds and reds that are being replaced by an indigo blue. I put my hands on the window pane. There, across the street, hid among a cluster of trees, is a place that scares me. I have heard the adults talking about it, and I have seen the people who live there, all clad in white and walking behind their minders with their heads bent, through the open field that separates our apartment building from the sea. They are the inmates of the mental hospital after which the street on which we live is named. Though I am only four years old I can sense their brokenness, and how their bodies have become shells from which their spirits have fled, as though the very life force has been sucked out of them.

But that is not what I am looking at now. I am watching the cars down on the street, their tops illuminated by the glow of the street lamps as they pass. More to the point: I am waiting for a bus to appear up ahead, for it to come to a stop near our building, and for my father to step out and to stroll towards the entrance, his feet turned slightly outward, briefcase in hand. All day I have been waiting for him to come home from his job at the bank so I can hop into his arms, bury my face in his neck, feel the rough tweed of his overcoat against my cheek.

Today I have been at home with my mother, like most days. I watched her on the floor, sitting with legs outstretched before her, alternating each leg forward as she crawled along the carpet on her behind. When I asked what she was doing, she said she was doing her exercises. When I asked why, she said it was to stay in shape. This told me nothing. There is much about my mother I do not understand. She is always doing something odd. For instance, when she finished her floor exercises, she took paper bits and laid them on top of fabric, affixed the paper with pins, then cut the fabric according to those shapes. Next, she took paint that had a strong, astringent smell and painted designs onto the fabric. When I asked her what she was doing, she said she was making a dress. When I asked her why she was painting the dress, she said she didn't want to have a dress like everyone else, she wanted a unique dress.

My mother is a source of endless wonder. I feel as though I am watching a beautiful creature behind a pane of glass who does all sorts of amazing things. Most of the time it's like she does not really notice what I am up to, like I'm simply a random observer of her various escapades. It's subtle, this remoteness she has; hard to pinpoint. She goes through the business of taking care of me–helping me get dressed, cooking oatmeal for my breakfast, telling me to wash my hands, setting down the bowl in front of me–but it's as though her mind is perpetually occupied with something beyond the here-and-now. I want her to see me, so I clamour for her attention: climbing on the sofa, jumping down, hopping on one leg the whole way through the kitchen–in from the hall side, out through the living room side–but she barely notices, and when I call "mamma, look!" she just gets annoyed and tells me to calm down, to go into the other room and play with my plastic farm animals.

I don't think my mother likes me very much.

My father's different. He plays games with me, takes me on piggy-back rides, and explains things so that I understand them. For instance, I wish we could have a television because my favourite time of the week is 6 p.m. on Sundays when there's a special kids' programme on. I don't always get to watch it, though, because to do so means going to someone else's house during the broadcast. My mother says we can't have a TV because the single Icelandic TV channel broadcasts only from 6 p.m. to 11 p.m. at the latest, there is no television on Thursdays, and none for the whole month of July. "What's the point of getting a TV just for that?" she says dismissively.

My father, on the other hand, says we *can* have one, but that he wants to buy a *colour* TV and right now the broadcasts are not in colour, only in black and white. This is confusing. How can a TV be in colour? "In the same way everything around us is in colour. And like when you colour something in your colouring book." Ah, okay. He lifts me up, carries me into the kitchen, grabs a chair that he puts in front of the wall oven, which has a window in the middle, and sets me on it. "There," he says grinning, "just watch that window and pretend you're watching TV". I look at him and scowl. Then he picks me up again and blows raspberries into my neck until I start giggling uncontrollably.

Now I'm waiting for him to come home … and here's the bus now, approaching the stop! I do some jumping on the spot in front of the window and ponder rushing down all the flights of stairs to greet him at the door, but decide against it because he might be in the elevator by the time I get down there. Below, in the distance, I hear the front door open and close, and a moment later there's the sound of it lurching into motion. I stand watching the green elevator door with its long and narrow frosted window in the middle, beyond which I can see the vague movement of cables, the thought of which always makes me uneasy because what if one of them snaps–or *all* of them snap–when someone's in there? It doesn't bear thinking about.

Finally, there's a line of solid darkness, and then light as the elevator reaches the landing. A click, then the door is pushed open and my *pabbi* steps through. He beams a smile when he sees me, scoops me up, and carries me up the flight of stairs and into our apartment. The sense of being a distant observer of things I don't understand, the feeling of not being noticed–both are swept away by the arrival of my father. It is as though all sounds and colours were muted, but now I can see, and hear, and feel.

I was five when I was summoned to the kitchen to hear the news that would upend everything. My father no longer worked at the bank–he'd decided to become an actor and had quit his day job. My mother, too, had decided to become an actress, and after they'd studied and graduated, one year apart, from Iceland's only acting school, they'd both embarked on careers in the theatre. My mother, I later learned, had initially been given plenty of opportunities, landing big roles in one or two major productions ... but then the work had dried up for her. My father, meanwhile, had formed his own theatre company with some friends, and they'd begun staging their own productions.

I perched on a stool at the end of the kitchen table with my favourite teddy bear in my arms, while they sat opposite one another–my mother with her hair swept up in a bun and her eyes lined like Cleopatra's; my father in a white shirt open at the neck, with the sleeves rolled up.

My pabbi cleared his throat, and began. My mamma and I, he pronounced, were going on a fantastical adventure. My aunt Klara, who lived in Canada with her Canadian husband and their three-year-old son Björn, was going to have another baby. Klara had asked my mother to come and help her, and my mother had said yes. I would be going along.

I looked from my father to my mother. Her beautiful face was impassive, while his forehead was crinkled, like it always was when he was worried. Yet it was the forced cheerfulness in his voice that I found most alarming.

"No," I said. "I want to stay with you."

He shifted in his chair. My mother sat perfectly still.

"You can't," he said. "I have to work."

"Your father is going on tour," said my mother. Even though she directed this at me, I could tell that she was really talking to him. My mother was not a part of his theatre company–the one with which he was now going on tour.

"I don't want to go there," I said.

My father leaned towards me. "You have no idea how lucky you are," he said in a conspiratorial tone, "it's *hot* there, and really sunny. You'll get to do all kinds of fun things."

"Like what?"

"All kinds of things," he repeated.

That's when I knew he was lying, because my father always explained things to me, but in this instance, he explained nothing.

To my five-year old mind, Canada was little more than a residential neighbourhood with tall trees and lush green grass, especially down by the Rideau Canal where the weeping willows hung their sad branches into the scummy green water.

Klara, her husband Jim, and my cousin Björn–nicknamed Billy–lived in a city called Ottawa, in a house made of red bricks with a grey wooden porch and a small lawn in front. Next door there lived a boy who was very fat, and who had an amazing collection of toys that you could scoot on down the driveway: two tricycles, a plastic turtle, a fire truck, and a tractor. I'd sit on the porch and watch him rolling back and forth on whatever gadget struck his fancy that day, making shouting noises in a language that I didn't understand.

My father was right about the sun shining. It really did shine, all the time, and the heat was relentless. He'd been wrong about the fun, though. I was not having fun. I was miserable. I hated the long afternoons of blazing heat, the humidity that made me so tired, and the mosquitos that sucked my blood and left bites that itched like crazy.

Back in Iceland there were no mosquitos.

I couldn't wait to go home to the cool breeze; to the big abandoned shipwreck at the shore across the road from our apartment building, where the neighbourhood kids went to play pirates; to my grandfather's garden, where he grew strawberries in the summer and always gave me the first ripe one. I loved that garden, especially when the entire family gathered there on sunny days.

But instead, there were slow meanderings behind my mother and big-bellied Klara down by the river, the forced isolation that came with not understanding what others were saying when they spoke English, and the big, scary monster of Things Unsaid.

We were sitting at a dressing table and my mother was brushing my hair.

"When are we going home, mamma?"

She yanked the brush. "Soon," she said, working to free it. "After Klara's had the baby."

"When's that going to be?"

"I don't know. Soon."

She was impatient with me. Every time I asked the question, or even talked about home, the Things Unsaid monster would appear.

Finally, Klara went into the hospital. My mother sidestepped into the role of homemaker and I helped as best I could, keeping watch over Billy while she made meals in the kitchen, helping her to set the table. A few days later Klara and Jim pulled up in their car with my new cousin in a carrier basket. I waited out on the porch with my mother and Billy, giddy with excitement–partly because I was excited to meet the baby, who had been given the name Sara, but mostly because this meant we could finally go home.

But we did not go.

The hazy summer turned to cooler days, the leaves on the trees changed colour, and we were still there. I was racked with frustration: I couldn't understand what we were doing there, now that the original mission for the trip had been fulfilled.

Then, just before Christmas, my mother announced that the time had come: we were leaving. I received the news warily–something in the way my mother and Klara stopped talking every time I entered a room told me something was going on to which I was not privy. It had to do with Jim and his new job, it seemed, which was in a faraway country called Cyprus. Jim was going to be working for something called United Nations, helping to build bridges and dams. As it turned out, it was not just my mother and me who were leaving Canada–Klara and Jim were, too, with my cousins. For now, Jim was going on ahead to Cyprus, while my mother, Klara, Sara, Billy and I were going to Iceland for Christmas.

Unbeknownst to my five-year-old self, my parents' marriage hung by a thread. While we were in Canada they had been writing passionate, torment-filled letters to each other about their feelings and the future of their relationship. Unable to reach a decision about whether or not to stay together, they decided to see when they were reunited in Iceland if their union could be salvaged. If yes, my mother and I would remain in Iceland with my father. If no, the two of us would go on to Cyprus with Klara and the children.

We returned to Iceland in early December, when the land is swathed in midwinter darkness and the light is crystalline. At that time of year, the days are almost entirely made up of dawn and dusk, each lasting for hours. There was snow on the ground, and the crisp tang of cool air filled my lungs when I breathed. My father was away with his theatre company when we arrived, and my mother decided that the two of us would fly up north to Akureyri to join him.

We landed in the early evening when my father was at the theatre, so my mother and I took a taxi to the small hotel where he was staying. She seemed tense and distracted, but also had a glow about her like someone nurturing hope. We checked in at reception, then ascended a narrow flight of stairs to my father's room on the third floor. It was warm and tranquil, with a dormer window facing the street, and a single lit lamp on a table in the corner. There was a double bed, and a smaller cot up against the wall. The air was thick with anticipation as my mother and I waited. There was no television to distract us, and no radio. We spoke in hushed voices, almost whispering, as though both of us were keenly aware of the fragility of this evening and its power to determine our future. An alarm clock on the bedside table ticked away the minutes. My mother said I needed to get into pyjamas and brush my teeth, and that I should try to fall asleep, but I knew I wouldn't be able to. I'd been waiting too many months to see my father again, and was determined to be awake when he got there.

Finally, there was the sound of a car outside. I rushed to the window, as I had rushed to the window at the sound of every car that had stopped outside the hotel since we checked in. It was him. From the window I saw him get out of the car, along with two other people. They exchanged a few words before he bounded up the front steps. I was beside myself with excitement. "It's him!" I shouted in a whisper, "it's him!" My mother took my arm. "Shhh," she said quietly, "let's listen to his footsteps on the stairs." I stopped. I listened. I heard them. Then the door opened. He dropped his bag and took two rapid steps towards my mother, and they embraced, tightly, turning in a circle, my father lifting my mother slightly off the ground. Then he released her, looked into her face, and they kissed. I could not contain myself any longer. I jumped up and down on the bed, howling. My father disengaged from my mother and came to me smiling. I leapt into his arms, felt them close around me, and at last I was home.

Evidently my parents' happy reunion did not extend much beyond that initial elation. About a week after we came back I learned that my mother and I would, in fact, be travelling with Klara and the children to Cyprus. The next thing I remember was sitting with my father on the sofa at my grandparents' house, my departure imminent. I was there to say goodbye. I did not want to go; I wanted to stay with him and with my grandparents. I was distraught. My father hugged me to him in an effort to comfort me, but it was no use–I refused to be consoled. Suddenly, as though the thought had just hit him, he exclaimed: "Hey! Did you know they have monkeys in the trees over there?"

I stopped weeping and looked at him.

"Did you know that?" he repeated.

I shook my head. I knew what he was trying to do. It was the same trick he had played when he said I was going to Canada and would have so much fun. I wasn't going to fall for that again. Even though I thought monkeys were awesome, especially the ones that sat on your shoulder, like Pippi Longstocking's monkey. My father had been reading the story of Pippi to me, and I longed to have a monkey just like hers.

"What kind of monkeys?" I mumbled, sniffling and wiping my nose.

"Monkeys. Little ones–you know. The cute little ones with the long tails."

"Like Pippi's?"

"Yes! Exactly like hers. What was his name again?"

"Mr. Nilsson," I said.

"That's right. Mr. Nilsson. They're everywhere in the trees over there, you can just take them home. I wish I could go over there and get myself a monkey." He paused. "Wait! I have an idea. Maybe you can get one for me. What do you think?"

I nodded, pressing my face against the side of him, inhaling his smell.

"Fantastic! You go get me a monkey."

My mother, Klara, my cousins and I arrived in Cyprus after a long journey that included an overnight bus trip from Amsterdam to Belgium, and a second overnight layover in Athens, Greece, where Jim came to meet us. When we landed in Nicosia, Jim drove us to the house that had been provided for him and Klara. It was a whitewashed bungalow with a red tile roof, red window shutters, and a fenced-off yard. I paid special attention to the trees. In the yard there were two tall ones with a proliferation of small green oval globes growing on them, slightly hairy, that I later learned were unripened almonds. There was a lemon tree right outside the kitchen window, and a small clementine tree against the corner of the fence that bordered the street.

While the adults busied themselves with unpacking, I went out to inspect the yard. I stared intently through the branches of the two almond trees, since those seemed by far the most likely to hold monkeys. When Klara came outside, she found me at the base of one of them, face turned upward.

"What are you doing?" she asked.

"Where are the monkeys?" I said. I was beginning to get a sinking feeling, like I suspected I'd been duped but didn't want to believe it.

"What monkeys?"

"The monkeys that are everywhere in the trees."

Klara shook her head. "There are no monkeys here. They have monkeys in India maybe, but not here."

She turned and went into the house. I sank down on my haunches against the trunk of the tree. So it was true–my father had lied to me. On purpose.

I let my chin drop to my chest.

Unless ... well, unless he didn't know. Maybe he just *thought* there were monkeys, but didn't know for sure. I would have to break the news to him that his dream of having a monkey was not going to come true. Unless Klara was wrong. Yes–maybe Klara was wrong. Perhaps I would see monkeys in the trees tomorrow, or the next day. Perhaps they were just extremely rare around here, but would materialise in time, and then I would be able to tame one and take it home.

But Klara was not wrong. In the 18 months we lived in Cyprus, I saw not a single monkey.

Dry, exotic, excruciatingly hot. Excursions to beaches with sand so blistering that it burned the soles of our feet; picnics in mountains dotted with tiny villages and castle ruins. Cats that ran wild, and cockroaches that flew. Grasshoppers the length of my hand. Going to the church across the street with my friend Christina, who lived in the house behind us, and staring wide-eyed at the lavish garments of the priest and the large lantern filled with incense that he swung back and forth as he chanted. Lining up with the pious churchgoers and kissing the image of Jesus on all the paintings.

("Ugh," Klara remarked to my mother when I told them. "Just think of the germs." I had not thought of the germs.) Barbed wire, and soldiers with guns on the tops of buildings. We lived in the Greek part, but sometimes went over to the Turkish section, where there were many poor people. During one such excursion we came upon a beggar, dirty and feral, who had lost both of his legs below the knee and was crawling along the street with blocks of wood attached to his stumps. As we passed, he looked up at us and extended a hand for spare change. His hair was wild, his beard unkempt. I had never before seen a person so stripped of human dignity, and the memory of him haunted me for years.

I had just turned six when we arrived, then I turned seven. It felt like my life was on hold, like it was an overcoat hung on a hook and promptly forgotten. I missed my father and the emotional nourishment he provided–nourishment that was not forthcoming on this faraway island that felt like a universe away. I had a sense of my spirit shrivelling up, becoming parched as the Cyprian ground in the summer heat. Sun, sand, daytime parties on sprawling estates that bordered the ocean; in the evenings the adults drinking wine and sometimes singing loudly. Like our previous stay in Canada, this time seemed to have no end. It was extended. And extended again. There was talk that I should be starting school–but then there didn't seem to be much point if we were going to be leaving soon. But we never seemed to leave.

Then, with very little preamble, it came: the announcement that we were going back to Iceland. I'd grown so distrustful of such declarations that I tempered my joy–but this time it was true. Our things were packed into boxes, I said goodbye to Christina and the white church across the street, then we boarded a flight to London, another one to Iceland, and at last we were home.

CHAPTER 2

IT WAS JUNE WHEN we came back–the season of glorious nights and perpetual daylight. My mother and I settled temporarily into an apartment that belonged to my maternal grandmother, Ella. Her husband–my mother's father–had died years earlier, when my mother was a little girl. I knew very little about him, except that he had been exceptionally good at drawing. One of his charcoal pieces had hung on the wall in our old apartment. Later I would learn more: that he'd been an alcoholic, and violent when drunk. He and my grandmother had had six children, and my mother was the youngest. They had separated when my mother was an infant, and he had died four years later of consumption.

My grandmother's apartment was in the basement of a three-storey house at the end of a cul-de-sac, and we would live there, my mother said, until we could move back into our other apartment–the one we had lived in with my father. Which I took to mean that we would move back in there *with* my father.

I expected him to meet us at the airport, but he didn't. Then I expected him to come to the apartment, but he didn't do that, either. This was confusing and upsetting. Where was he? We'd been away for what seemed like forever–why had he not been there to greet us? And my grandparents–where were they? I asked my mother and she said that my father now lived in Akureyri, the same town we'd flown to when we went to see him on tour. He would come, she said, just not *right now*. I wondered why he didn't call us on the phone, but thought better of asking … my mother was not forthcoming with information, and whenever we spoke of my father, I felt her grow tense. The same happened when I asked about seeing my grandparents. No, I could not go to their house. "Why not?" Because.

Then one morning, when we'd been in my grandmother's apartment for about a month, my mother told me that my father was coming that afternoon. I was overjoyed! He was coming at last!

"What time?" I demanded breathlessly.

"Three-thirty or four."

Oh no! I'd been invited to a girl's birthday party across the street. "But I'll be at the party!"

"I'll let you know when he gets here."

"I'm not going. I want to wait for him here," I declared.

"No. You will go to the party."

Her tone was such that I knew there was no point in arguing. Reluctantly I schlepped my sorry self across the street at 3 p.m. My mind resided somewhere outside my body, and it was impossible to take part in games since I had to keep running outside to see if my father was coming. While the kids played, rambunctious and loud, I stood on the front porch staring at the corner, as though I could manifest him out of thin air if I kept my gaze fixed on it hard enough. And … it worked! At last, a figure appeared, wearing a loose jacket, striding towards me, feet turned slightly outward. I knew that stride immediately. Bounding down the steps I ran towards him and threw myself into his embrace. I'd spent eighteen months thinking about him and trying to conjure up what he looked like, and now he was here, *finally* here.

He hugged me, then set me down and we walked to the apartment together. My mother was standing at the door, stiffly, as though she'd been waiting.

"Go back to the birthday party while your father and I talk," she said to me.

I was about to protest, but he spoke first. "Why can't she stay?" he asked.

My mother stood for a moment, then moved aside in silent concession. I went into the living room while they took a stand opposite one another in the kitchen, leaning against the U-shaped counter. I noticed that they'd not embraced–not like they had when we'd gone up north to see him that time. Moreover, they did not seem overly happy to be reunited. I wanted to show my father a drawing I'd made for him that morning, but on glancing at the two of them in the kitchen I decided I'd better not. Instead, I began building a house out of playing cards on the carpeted floor, a skill I'd been teaching myself. Alas, it kept collapsing, and I hoped my father would not come in and see how hopelessly inept I was at this. Finally, I gave up, lay down on the floor, and closed my eyes.

I don't know how much time passed, but when I woke up my father was on his haunches, touching my shoulder.

"Do you want to take a little walk?" he asked.

We went outside. The sun was so bright that it hurt my eyes. The birthday party had moved out into the street and the kids were running around and shouting, playing games in nearby gardens.

"Isn't there a place around here that sells ice cream?" he said.

"Over there," I said, gesturing.

We walked along a footpath to a small plaza. After getting our ice cream–soft cones, mine dipped in chocolate–we strolled slowly back the way we came. Stopping at a small playground, we took a seat on a bench.

"When are you going to come and live with us?" I asked him.

He hesitated for what seemed like a long time, then said: "Your mother and I are not going to live together anymore."

I did not understand. I had no conception of a future in which my mother and father did not live together.

"... But you can come stay with me sometimes," he added.

Stay? Who was this man? Was he not my father? My mother and I were finally back in Iceland. We were supposed to live with him, not go *stay* with him sometimes!

"Where are you going to live?" I asked. My voice sounded shrill.

"I live in Akureyri now. You can come to stay with me there." He was trying to sound upbeat, but it wasn't working–he just sounded tired.

"When?"

"Soon, I hope."

I looked down. A line of melted ice cream crept across the base of my thumb. This day had turned awful. Earlier I'd felt light and pretty; now I felt gawky and hideous. I'd felt like my father belonged to me and I to him; now he seemed like a stranger. The sun had felt warm on my skin; now I just felt cold. I extended my hand holding the rest of my cone. My father took it, and tossed it into a nearby trash bin. Then we walked back to the apartment.

That autumn, my mother and I moved back into our home near the sea in Reykjavík–the one we had previously lived in with my father. It belonged to me now, my mother said, which sounded bizarre, but she explained that she and my father had agreed to put it into my name so that she and I would always have a place to live.

It seemed smaller than before, with its single bedroom, living room, kitchen and bathroom. My mother and I shared the bedroom; my bed against one wall, hers against the other. She was still behind that pane of glass, distant and unreachable, even more so than before we left for Canada, when she had done her exercises on the floor and made her own clothes. I felt bereft and abandoned. I could no longer stand at the window and wait for the bus to deliver some light and warmth in the shape of my father. I was alone with my mother, who seemed locked in her own universe.

Now that we were back in Iceland, it was finally time for me to start school. I had never been, even though kids my age had started a year previously. On the first day of classes my mother had to work, so my grandmother Alda, whom I was named after, went with me. I held fast to her hand, anxious at what lay ahead–everyone would know each other, and I would be the new kid. While we waited at the office to find out where I was supposed to go, my grandmother struck up a conversation with a woman dressed in a chic skirt suit. A girl my age held her hand. She was also new. Through a bit of engineering on the part of my grandmother and her mother, this girl and I joined forces. We went to our new classroom together, sat side-by-side, and walked home after school. It was a comfort to have a friend, though it was clear to me that we would never be close. She lived with both her parents, and her mother was a stay-at-home mom. I came from a broken home, and was a latchkey kid. Shame was beginning to make its insidious imprint, and I felt unworthy of her friendship.

Since school was only for half a day, and since there was no one to take care of me in the mornings, I became a ward of a newfangled daycare institution, set up as an experiment by the City of Reykjavík to meet the needs of a growing number of single-parent families. The rate of divorce was going up in the late 1960s, yet failed marriages were still considered somewhat disgraceful. We who wore our keys around our necks were treated as suspect by the cookie-baking, stay-at-home moms of "good" families. This was brought sharply home one day when a friend invited me to her house to play after school. Her mother, who was initially very open and welcoming, turned reticent and wary when I disclosed that I was at the daycare centre up the road, of which she had evidently heard. There was something in her raised eyebrows and the way she said "ah" that instantly made me feel depraved and innately dirty. In retrospect I wonder if she thought her untainted, bourgeois daughter would become contaminated by an urchin like me, or perhaps she feared that whatever had happened in my household was infectious, and might happen within her perfect home, as well. Hard to say.

Yet perhaps it was not only the stigma I perceived from society that undermined my sense of self-worth. There was also something happening to my mother. She had never been the warm, nurturing type, but now she was growing hard and bitter. My father had always met me on my terms and given me permission to be a child, yet my mother seemed to require something else entirely, making constant, arbitrary demands that I sensed, but did not fully understand. All I knew was that when I failed to meet her expectations, she became disproportionately angry and punishing.

The first time it happened, I had failed to pick up my toys. I'd been playing with my plastic animal collection and some Legos that were a hand-me-down from a cousin, and they were spread all over the floor of our bedroom. My mother came in and told me to pick them up and put them away. I dawdled–lay down on my side and refused to comply. She became irate and asked if I wanted her to take all my toys, put them in a bag, and throw them in the garbage. Defiant, I told her to go ahead. She went into the kitchen and found a plastic bag, then came back to the bedroom and, pale with anger, scooped all my toys into the bag before marching out into the hallway and throwing it down the garbage chute. I watched her with growing panic, firmly resolved not to let her see the effect she was having on me, and not believing until the last moment that she would actually follow through. When she came back in, I laid down on the bed with a book I had been reading, and feigned nonchalance, though secretly devastated that my toys were gone. Later that evening I asked her if she would go down to the garbage room and get them, and promised I would not argue if she told me to pick up my toys again. She refused. I'd had my chance, she said, and now I had to live with the consequences.

I learned that my mother's temper was volatile and harsh, and I became perpetually afraid of upsetting her. I sensed that much of her anger had to do with my father, and made sure I never mentioned him. I pretended that he was barely on my radar, even though he was, and I missed him terribly. Sometimes she launched into acrimonious tirades about his "weak" character and all the offences he had committed against her. He had decided to go to acting school and left her at home with the baby (me); he had preferred his theatre friends over her; he was not a good husband to her (*why* was never entirely clear to me). These bursts of acrimony were spoken *at* me, not *to* me, yet I felt them as though they were barbed wire piercing my skin. I loved my father but kept silent, carrying her rancour like an obedient mule, feeling trapped by her evident presumption of my loyalty and a feeling of disgrace that I could not ascribe to anything.

As children–as *people*–we yearn to be seen. When our uniqueness and individuality is not recognised by the people who matter to us the most, it is like the flame we carry inside is slowly extinguished. I did not feel seen by my mother, and this feeling grew stronger with time.

Perhaps the most evident sign that I was invisible to her came one morning when I went to put on my favourite trousers–green corduroys that my father had bought for me, and which I wore all the time. Only, that day I couldn't find them. Finally, after a frantic search, I located them lying at the end of the sofa with a big tear in the bum.

"What happened to my trousers?" I asked my mother, panicked.

Looking abashed, she explained that two of her girlfriends had come over the previous evening and had seen my corduroys. One of them had held them up and asked my mother if she realised that her child was wearing clothes so worn that you could practically see through the fabric. My mother had protested that it was not so bad, at which her friend had challenged her to poke her finger into the seat of the trousers. My mother had done so, with the aforementioned result.

She had failed to notice that an item of clothing her child wore almost every day was threadbare to the point that a single poke would ruin it. Or perhaps she simply did not care–that is, until someone else noticed, and pointed out her shortcoming.

That day she gave me money and told me to go and buy myself a new pair of trousers.

I was eight years old, and had never gone shopping for anything for myself before. I wandered listlessly up and down Laugavegur, the main shopping street in Reykjavík, going into a couple of shops and checking out the trouser selection, feeling very conspicuous, thinking the staff would surely be wondering what a child my age was doing there all by herself. Besides, I didn't want a new pair of pants. What I wanted were the corduroys that my father had given me, because when I wore them, I felt like myself.

Those were hard years, when I felt myself being pulled into the dark chambers of my mother's rage–a vortex of terror, for I sensed that, at the heart of it, was something terrible: a place without love.

To me, that place manifested in the summer when I was eight years old. My mother arranged for me to stay with her brother and sister-in-law for the season in a small fishing village on Iceland's Snæfellsnes peninsula, while she worked at a country hotel about an hour's drive away. I do not know why I did not stay with my father or paternal grandparents, though I am guessing that some kind of arrangement was made between my mother and her brother and sister-in-law, because that winter their eldest daughter moved to the capital to attend school, and lived with us for a few months.

I did not know these relatives and could not remember having met them prior to being thrust upon them in this way. My uncle was a kind-hearted, if rather reticent, man who worked as a foreman at the town's fish processing plant; he went to work early in the mornings and returned home at dinnertime. His wife, who was a homemaker, had a cool and severe disposition, and made it fully clear that it had not been her wish to have her husband's stray niece dumped on her. She ignored me to the extent that she could, while doting on her own children–she and my uncle had four, of which two were at home. The room I slept in belonged to my cousin, who was a year younger than me, while he had the room of his older brother, who was away for the summer. I spent as much time as I could alone, finding solace in the Donald Duck comics that lined my cousin's bookshelf. My cousin resented me–why, I do not know; maybe he did not appreciate being ousted from his room, or he simply took a page from his mother's playbook. At any rate, he made a point of making my life miserable. He was hostile and contemptuous, and when he realised my affinity for the comic books he removed them from his room, saying I couldn't have them. He also found other ways to torment me, like kicking me under the table at mealtimes when his father was not home. When I complained to his mother, she reproached me for being a tattle-tale.

I felt desperately lonely and misunderstood, and lived for the infrequent phone calls from my mother. I would wait impatiently while she first talked to uncle or auntie, before the phone was passed to me. I wanted very much to pour out my heart to her and tell her how forlorn I felt, but the two of them were always within earshot and I could never speak my mind.

The prospect of spending the entire summer starved for love and warmth filled me with despair. It felt as though every drop of vibrancy and joy was being sucked out of me. *I can't do it*, I thought; *I will die*. And so, I crafted a plan.

My mother had left me with a little bit of pocket money that I wasn't quite sure how I was supposed to use, though I understood it was meant for emergencies. Frankly I could think of no greater emergency than the current situation, so one morning, with the omnipresent smell of fish lingering in the misty air, I slipped out of the house without anyone noticing and quickly made my way to the local Póstur og sími–Post and Telephone Office–on the edge of town, where a telephone call could be placed with the help of an operator.

I walked with my head down, feeling conspicuous as a thief, terrified that auntie would catch on to my plan and come after me, or that one of her friends in town would see me and alert her. Neither happened; I made it to the Póstur og sími without being apprehended, and pulled open the heavy front door. Inside all was quiet and orderly. There was a high writing desk for addressing envelopes, and against the wall two soundproof booths with telephones. A clerk sat behind a counter, busy with some paperwork. I cast around, anxious that someone might recognise me, but there was no one else there. Emboldened, I walked to the counter, which seemed inordinately high, and proffered the coins my mother had given me, asking the clerk to place a call to the hotel where she worked. The clerk–a woman–responded good-naturedly that I would have to fill out a form with the telephone number of the person I wanted to reach. This threw me into a panic, for I did not know the number of the hotel, only its name. Seeing my distress, the clerk asked me who I wanted to speak to, and I explained that I had to reach my mother who was working at the Hotel Búðir on the other side of the peninsula. The kind clerk directed me into one of the booths and told me to pick up the receiver and wait for my mother to come on the line, which I did. It took forever for the person at the hotel to locate her, but at long last I heard her voice. I had a huge lump in my throat and could hardly get the words out to say what I needed to say. I asked her to please come, saying I couldn't stay there a day longer because I was miserable. She was taken aback. I wanted her empathy, but instead she sounded mad. She had to work, she said–she couldn't just come and get me. I asked if I could go to Akureyri and stay with my father. She said no, that wasn't possible. What about my grandparents? No. Why wasn't it possible? It just wasn't.

My mother asked if auntie was there. Frantically I explained what I had done–that I was in the Póstur og sími–and begged her not to tell them that I had come out here and tattled on them. I was sure there would be repercussions if auntie knew.

Fifteen minutes after entering the Póstur og sími I left, feeling crestfallen. I had clung to the hope that my mother would rally to my aid, but she had been very dismissive. Eyes downcast, I walked back along the same road I had taken about twenty minutes earlier, then a determined little warrior. I felt utterly despondent.

Two nights later I was taking a bath when I heard a car pull up outside, then voices. It was ... it was my mother's voice!

Never I have jumped out of a bath so quickly. My mother was here! She had come! I was jubilant.

She was in the foyer, not yet out of her coat, and I threw myself into her arms. She hugged me, smiling, while continuing her conversation with my aunt and uncle, who were looking on. Auntie made some coffee and brought out refreshments–flatbread with smoked salmon, cream biscuits–and we all sat down at the kitchen table together. Auntie always changed when she was around my mother and now she became positively ingratiating, gazing at me with affected kindness and saying what a good girl I was and how well I got on with her children–even patting me on the shoulder, which she never did when no one was around. I could not believe how fake she was and felt outraged at her smarmy performance.

My mother had gotten a lift with a friend, who had already left. Since it was late, it was decided that she would stay the night, and my uncle offered to drive her back the following day–a Saturday. My cousin was evicted from his older brother's room, which had a twin bed, and sent back into his own room, so that my mother and I could sleep in the larger bed.

I was convinced that my mother had come to take me away. Indeed, no other thought crossed my mind, even when my uncle said that he would drive her back to the hotel the next day; so great was my yearning to get out of there. It was not until the following morning when my mother was getting dressed, that it became clear she had no intention of taking me with her. I would have to stay.

"I can't," I said with emphasis. "Please take me. Please!"

"How am I supposed to do that?" she retorted. "I live in a house that is just for staff. There are no kids allowed. Why do you think you're here?"

"No, mamma. Take me with you. Please," I begged.

"I can't!"

"Why can't I go stay with pabbi, then?"

"Because he doesn't want you."

Her words were like daggers. I clammed up instantly. She turned away and hooked up her bra.

"I'm not staying here," I said fiercely. "I'll run away."

She turned around, her expression dark. "You know what you are?" she snapped. "You are *selfish.* You think only of yourself."

She left the room. I stayed behind, paralysed with shame. I felt as though I couldn't move.

Time felt like it was passing with excruciating slowness. I felt devastated and utterly powerless. After what seemed like forever the door opened again. It was my mother. "Pack your things," she said abruptly.

I asked no questions, just went quickly into the other room and threw everything I had into my suitcase, my heart thrumming in my chest. When I came out, holding my case, auntie made a sad face. "Are you leaving us already?"

It was a strange day. We went on an outing to a beach that had red sand and lots of shells. My mother barely spoke to me. Uncle and auntie were the same as they always were with people outside their immediate family, though I detected some relief from auntie that I was off her hands.

Even though no children were allowed, my mother did take me with her to the workers' quarters at the hotel. For the next two days I was surreptitiously kept in the room my mother shared with two other women, who were friendly to me and did not blow the whistle. During the day my mother went to the hotel to work, and I played outside among the sand dunes and the lava, taking care to stay out of sight. On the third day someone drove us to a nearby town, from which my mother and I and a woman who worked with her caught a bus back to Reykjavík.

My mother did not go back to work at the hotel. The pay had been bad, she said, and the working conditions unsatisfactory. Instead, she went to work for her brother–a different one–at his silk printing workshop in downtown Reykjavík. I was intensely relieved to be home, but somewhere, deep inside, I felt changed. My mother's words had been planted in my subconscious, and I could not erase them: *You are selfish. You think only of yourself. Your father doesn't want you.* My guilt was overwhelming, and I believed she was right–I was selfish, and I had been very, very bad to demand her protection.

Yet although my mother could be neglectful, even cruel, there were times when she stepped up for me. Such as when I was eight and my homeroom teacher called to inform my mother that I had stopped doing my math homework, and was at the risk of failing math class. Humiliated and full of shame I had to admit to her that this was absolutely true, that I did not understand math, and had therefore stopped doing the homework.

"But what about the tutor at the daycare?" she asked.

The daycare centre hired a tutor who came in daily to help us kids with our homework. He was an older man–a retired former schoolteacher. There was a room on the upper floor with a couple of long tables and some chairs, where we did our schoolwork. But lately the tutor had started making me uneasy. Something about the way he closed the door when he was tutoring me, when it was just me and him in the room. He had also started sitting right up against me and putting his arm around me, squeezing me to him like he was my grandfather or something. I didn't like it. I didn't like *him.*

Yet I didn't tell my mother that. I simply shrugged and said I hadn't wanted to do the homework, at which she ordered me to sit down and not get up until I had finished all the assignments I had failed to hand in over the last several weeks.

Even though I muddled through the assignments, I was no closer to understanding what I was doing. And so, I reluctantly went to see the tutor at the daycare. It seemed that I was always alone with him these days–perhaps he chose a time to see me when the other children were out, or at school. At any rate, he shut the door, then came and sat next to me. Bending over my notebook, he put his arm around my waist and pulled me to him, so that I was sitting on his lap. He kissed the side of my face near my temple. I felt nauseous, yet trapped–unable to move. "What's this?" he said, leaning in, rubbing his thumb over something on the back of my hand. It was nothing, just a teeny-tiny red mark, certainly nothing that troubled me. I shrugged and said I didn't know, my mind churning to figure out how I could extricate myself from this situation. He rubbed it some more and asked me if it hurt. I shook my head. Then he brought my hand up to his lips and kissed the red mark he considered so serious, letting his lips linger so that I writhed in disgust.

Just then I heard footsteps on the stairs outside the door. I leapt off his lap and mumbled that I had to go. Then I grabbed my books and ran from the room.

That evening, while I was doing my homework, I kept looking at the red mark on my hand. It was just a pinprick that I had never given a second thought before. When I was finished, I went to my mother and held up my hand, asking her what the mark was. She glanced indifferently at it, then leaned closer.

"What mark?"

I pointed it out to her. It was hard to see.

She shrugged. "I don't think it's anything."

"Is it dangerous?"

"Dangerous?" She looked at it again. "No. It's just a little discolouration of your skin. Why?"

"The tutor at the daycare was asking me about it. He took me on his lap and kissed it."

"He what?"

I explained.

She stared straight ahead, and was so still that I thought she might not have heard me. Then she looked at me and said, "Do not go into a room with that man again."

The next day I was just finishing lunch at the daycare when I heard a familiar voice in the front foyer. I jumped up from the table and, amazed, saw my mother disappearing into the office of the director, a buxom woman named Jóhanna. I turned away, racked with anxiety: Was she going to tell on me? Would she repeat what I had told her about the tutor? He'd be mad. And everyone would … everyone would know that I had been in there alone with him and had sat on his lap.

I hung around the foyer, fidgety and scared. About fifteen minutes later my mother emerged, said goodbye to Jóhanna, put her hand on my shoulder, and said she'd see me that evening. Jóhanna looked grim. She asked me to come into her office, and asked if the tutor had taken me onto his lap. I said nothing, just stared at the brown linoleum floor. She came around her desk, sat down next to where I stood, and assured me that this was just between me and her–that she would not tell the tutor what I told her, but that she needed to know. I looked into her face, and saw that she meant it. Reassured, I repeated what I had told my mother.

Later that day the tutor was dismissed. I never saw him again. And to this day I am thankful that, despite all her previous and subsequent failings, my mother came to my aid in such a decisive and unhesitating manner.

CHAPTER 3

FOR AS LONG AS I could remember, I had dreamed of having a dog.

I loved everything about dogs. I loved the affection they gave; their boundless enthusiasm and energy; their unwavering loyalty. Jim and Klara had given me a book about dogs one Christmas, and I knew it almost by heart. I knew all the breeds and the qualities specific to them. My favourite was collie–I had watched Lassie every week at my friend Christina's house in Cyprus and that was the kind of dog I wanted because Lassie was good, and kind, and rescued people.

Yet there was a rather critical hitch. The city of Reykjavík had strict bylaws prohibiting dogs. For complex reasons involving a tapeworm epidemic centuries earlier, Icelanders distrusted dogs, and considered them dirty, disease-ridden beasts that belonged in the countryside with the peasants–not with sophisticated city dwellers. I would have given anything to make my dream a reality, but I also knew that my yearning for a dog would remain unfulfilled as long as we lived in Reykjavík.

Yet one day at school I accidentally heard the most remarkable thing. Two girls in my class were talking, and one mentioned her dog. I could hardly believe what I was hearing. Even though I felt timid around these girls–they were popular, I was not–I went directly to where they were standing and demanded to know if this was true–if she really owned a dog. A real, live dog.

"Yeah," she replied, evidently taken aback by my boldness.

"What kind?"

She glanced at her friend. "Maltese," she said.

"Can I see it?" I said.

Again she glanced at her friend, who raised her eyebrows. Turning back to me she shrugged, and said sure, I could walk home with her after school if I wanted.

I don't recall her name, only that she had long, blonde hair and very dainty feet. I knew she was totally out of my league as a friend, and anyway, that was not what I was after. I just needed to see that dog. After school I waited while she chatted conspiratorially with another girl, and watched her put on her boots, coat, mitts and hat, all of which matched perfectly. She waved goodbye to her friend, cast a glance at me, and headed to the exit as I kept awkward pace beside her. She lived on one of the swankier streets in the neighbourhood, in a detached family home with a garden, about a ten-minute walk away. When we reached her house, she pointed to one of the windows, and oh! there it was: a tiny ball of bustling fur, watching us intently. A moment later it vanished from view, only to come bounding out through the front door towards us. The girl's mother stood in the doorway, beaming. "Hi Snotra, hey girl," my classmate pealed, leaning down to scoop up the pooch, kissing and nuzzling the top of its head as she trod lightly up the garden lane. I remained standing on the sidewalk, dazzled by the Disney-esque perfection of this scene. She did not turn to say goodbye, just vanished through the door like she had forgotten all about me.

I remained on the sidewalk for a moment, then headed back in the direction from which we had come, my head full of thoughts about this wondrous discovery I had just made. Maybe since my classmate had a dog, I could have one, too. Would I be able to hide it from the authorities while living in the apartment building with my mother? It would be difficult, surely. Unless I took the dog out only at night, when people were asleep. But then I wouldn't be able to sleep, myself ... and I had to go to school. But what if I lived somewhere else, like in my paternal grandparents' house, where there was a garden ...?

I stopped. It was only a couple of blocks to my grandparents' house, I realised. Maybe instead of going to the daycare place, which I did not particularly like, I could go there. Just to check if someone was home. My grandmother worked every second day as an x-ray technician at a health clinic, and with any luck, I thought, this would be one of her days off.

I turned, and began walking in that direction.

My grandparents' house was about a ten-minute walk from where my mother and I lived, on a quiet street lined with two-storey houses, some of which were single-family homes, and some of which contained two or more apartments. The houses all had gardens, and the man who lived in the downstairs apartment across the street from them even had a stable in his yard, where he kept a horse. My grandparents lived in a one-bedroom apartment on the upper floor of a house that they had built, and owned another on the ground floor, in which my mother, father and I had lived when I was a baby. It was now occupied by my uncle B.

"Oh, hello!" exclaimed my grandmother when she opened the front door. She appeared both surprised and delighted. "What are you doing here? Shouldn't you be at your daycare?"

"I just wanted to see if anyone was home because I walked

home with a girl I know and she lives not far away," I explained somewhat incoherently.

"Okay," she said.

"Can I do my homework here?"

She hesitated, then said: "Sure. But you'll have to call your mother and ask. She'll have to let the daycare people know."

I called my mother and she gave permission for me to stay. In the kitchen my grandmother buttered two slices of bread, topped one with egg and tomato and the other with liver paté, then put both in front of me with a glass of milk. She sat down at the table and lit a cigarette. As I ate, I asked how it was possible for a girl in my class to have a dog since they were illegal. She said that not everyone obeyed the law and that if the girl's family got caught with a dog they would be in trouble. "What would happen?" I wanted to know. She explained that they would have to pay a fine, and maybe the dog would be taken away.

That did not sound good.

Next she asked me how school was going. I said I was learning to write in longhand, and showed her how it was done. I went into the dining room and did my homework, then lay on the sofa and read a book. It was a wonderful afternoon, and I decided I would do this more often if my grandmother agreed.

My grandmother did agree. From that day onward my visits to my grandparents' house became more frequent. Soon I had my own key, and since I spent so much time there my mother and grandmother deemed it unnecessary to keep paying for my place at the daycare. Someone was always at home in one of the other apartments in the house, even if my grandmother was at work, and I made friends with a boy and girl next door–siblings, who were a little older and a little younger than me, respectively. We would play inside the little hallway that connected the apartments, or join other kids in the neighbourhood for outdoor games.

The garden on the south side of the house, which belonged

to my grandparents and which my grandfather tended with great care, had beautiful summer flowers, rowan and evergreen trees, redcurrant bushes, and a verdant lawn. Yet his pride and joy were his strawberries. They are a challenge to grow in Iceland's cold climate, but every summer my grandfather managed it. He also gave me my very own set of redcurrant bushes that I cherished, especially in late summer when they bore lovely, red, tart berries that were picked and made into jelly by my grandmother. When my grandfather came home from work, I accompanied him into the garden where he taught me to pull weeds, trim the edges of flowerbeds, and rake the freshly-cut grass into rows. When the grass was dry, he carted it in a wheelbarrow to his neighbour across the street, who fed it to his horse. In return the neighbour sometimes let me sit on the horse's back, walking me slowly up and down my grandparents' driveway while I grinned like a lunatic. I desperately wanted a horse of my own, but like the dog it was a distant dream, far beyond the scope of what seemed possible.

Yet it was not all effervescent sunshine at my grandparents' house. My grandfather struggled with alcoholism. Every few months, his addiction–that cunning trickster–would whisper that surely he could handle "just one". He could not. That one drink invariably turned into an uncontrolled bout of drinking that lasted days, and sometimes weeks. My grandmother took care of him, calling his place of employment–an accounting firm–to say he could not come to work, sitting up with him nights as he drank and ranted, and making trips to the liquor store for him. That last part was always contentious, and many people heartily disapproved–yet my grandmother knew that if she did not go, my grandfather would find other ways to source his booze. He would call his drinking buddies to come over, or phone one of the so-called "good" taxis that illicitly sold booze to desperate men like him, charging four or five times the amount that state-run liquor stores did–an amount that was already ridiculously high. During these episodes, while my *afi* was "sick", I was barred from visiting. On one or two occasions I witnessed him in this state, but generally I was sheltered from his condition until he had transformed from the frightful Mr. Hyde back into a benign and friendly Dr. Jekyll.

My grandparents had an upright piano, which my grandfather sometimes played. He and my grandmother also had a collection of classical records, most of them featuring piano music. I had started to pick at the notes of the piano, trying to replicate some of the music I heard on those records. My favourite was the Adagio of Mozart's Piano Concerto No. 21. Through endless trial and error, I finally figured out the melody, and one day in late October my grandfather came home from work to find me playing. He sat down on the piano bench next to me, and watched.

"You should be taking lessons," he said.

"Isn't it expensive?"

My grandfather looked at my grandmother, who had come into the room without me noticing. "Yes," she said, "but if you really want to learn, I am sure we can work something out."

"You would have to practice, though," my grandfather said. "You'd have to come here every day after school."

I brightened. Nothing would suit me better than to have an excuse to spend more time at my grandparents'. I gravitated towards them because there I found the light and the conditions I needed to grow.

A few blocks away, where I lived with my mother, life felt impossibly hard. It was filled with shadows that were invisible to outsiders, and which I was unable to understand. There was something in the way she interacted with me that was deeply hurtful, and which I registered in my subconscious and in my body, more than on any conscious level. I do not believe it was her intention to be cruel, but it is evident to me now that she was afflicted with a personality disorder that she kept carefully hidden behind a façade of competence and charisma. She appeared to outsiders as a loving mother, yet her demands on me were harsh and often impossible for a young child to fulfil.

My mother's older sister Alma had four daughters–the two youngest with her husband. The elder, Hrefna, was six months older than I was, and in contrast to me lived an exceedingly sheltered life. I was used to taking the bus across town, being home alone, and generally fending for myself. Not so Hrefna. She was adored by her parents, and especially her father–an affluent businessman perpetually ready to open his purse to fulfil his daughter's whims.

One evening in early November, when I was eight and Hrefna nine, I overheard my mother on the phone with Alma making arrangements for Hrefna and me to spend the following day together. Alma had some errands to run, and Hrefna could not be left at home by herself. I groaned inwardly. I didn't much care for my cousin. It was hard to get her to engage. Whenever I asked her something–say, whether she wanted to go to the ice cream shop to check if they had any broken cones to give away–she'd just grin sheepishly and not really answer, though she would follow me to the shop and help me eat the cones if there were any. At the time she was considered a little introverted; today she would probably be diagnosed with some type of disorder.

The plan, as cooked up by our mothers, was for Hrefna and me to meet at the Hlemmur bus station downtown, and then go to a nearby swimming pool. For Icelanders, outdoor thermal pools serve as de facto community centres. There is one in every settlement in Iceland that has access to geothermal heat, and every neighbourhood of the capital Reykjavík has its own pool. People go to the pools not only to exercise, but to play with their children, meet their friends and neighbours, and discuss politics and current affairs. Children as young as ten can go to the pools unsupervised, though at that time the age limit was eight.

Hrefna and I met as planned, but quickly discovered that neither one of us had any interest in going to the pool. So, we did the only reasonable thing: bought candy for the admission money and wandered around downtown. The Reykjavík city centre is not large, and in those days I roamed the area frequently, especially if I was hanging out at the silk printing workshop that belonged to my mother's brother, and where she worked.

As usual, Hrefna and I were not really communicating, and moping around downtown got tedious. By 4 p.m. it had started to get dark. I was beginning to feel cold and wanted to go to my grandparents'–my perpetual refuge. Hrefna agreed to come with me, but by the time we were on the bus to my grandparents' we were bickering about something. Irritated with her, I decided to move up a couple of rows. The bus drove on and soon approached the stop where we would disembark. I rang the bell to signal that I wanted to get off, then stood up. Hrefna did the same. We stood at the rear door of the bus, not speaking, and when the bus came to a stop we both got off. I headed in the direction of my grandparents' house, expecting Hrefna to follow.

When I got to the corner where we would turn, I glanced around to make sure Hrefna was behind me. She was not. In fact, she was nowhere to be seen.

No. Oh no. I knew I would be in trouble if I didn't find her, for even though Hrefna was older than me, my mother had made it perfectly clear that she was my responsibility. I looked all around, then doubled back to the bus stop to see if I could see her anywhere.

Nothing.

Panicked, dreading what might happen if I didn't find Hrefna, I ran to my grandparents', hoping that by some freakish means she would have found her way there on her own–exceedingly wishful thinking, since Hrefna had never been to my grandparents' house. I explained to my grandmother what had happened, and she went and roused my uncle B who was the only one in the family who owned a car. B, who was very tall, folded himself into his little Austin Mini, I got in next to him, and together we combed the neighbourhood, looking for Hrefna.

By now it was dark, and the wind had picked up. It had also started to snow. Unable to find my cousin we went back to my grandparents', and my grandmother called my mother on the phone. I looked on, trembling, for I knew my mother would be livid. Fifteen minutes later she arrived at my grandparents' house, her face tight with anger, and demanded to know how, exactly, I had managed to lose Hrefna. Her parents had been informed, she told me, and they were hysterical with worry. Everyone was out searching for her. I sat in the chair in my grandparents' hallway, shrinking with every word, wishing I could vanish.

My mother and B went out in his car to continue searching while I sat motionless in the chair, heartsick and scared. My grandmother came, gave me a squeeze, and offered me some cookies, which I declined. I don't know how long it was–maybe half an hour, maybe an hour–before I heard the sound of B's Mini outside. I looked anxiously at my mother and B as they came in, and was relieved to see that they appeared a good deal more lighthearted than when they had left. Hrefna, it transpired, had been found. She had shown a fortitude no one thought she had, and much to everyone's amazement had made her own way home on foot.

There was relief all around, and though my mother chatted amiably enough with my grandmother and B, I could tell that she was furious with me. I held out weak hope that I might be able to stay at my grandparents'–to have dinner with them and even spend the night–but I knew it would not happen. No way would my mother permit anything that might be construed as a reward for what I had done.

Gloomily I dressed in my boots and jacket and trudged down the steps of my grandparents' house after my mother. As soon as we were out of eye- and earshot, she turned and hissed between clenched teeth: *Þú ert fjölskyldunni til skammar.* "You are a disgrace to this family."

Her words were like the lashing of a whip. With my child's perception, so indelibly coloured by hers, I could not but agree that she was right. I had done something deplorable. I *was* a disgrace. There was not a doubt in my mind that Hrefna's parents thought so, too, and that from this evening forward I would be a pariah in my mother's family. Not only had I humiliated her brother and sister-in-law by demanding to be removed from their home, I had failed to look after my older cousin and keep her safe.

The certainty that every relative on my mother's side felt me to be a disgrace to the family stayed with me well into my adult years, and coloured every interaction I had with them. In hindsight I realise that they probably thought no such thing–that they likely had very few thoughts of me at all. Yet my child's heart believed that I had committed a heinous crime, and I carried the burden of that transgression for years to come. It would be decades before I fully understood that to expect of a child what my mother had expected of me was delusional, and the fact that she considered me a disgrace had everything to do with her own projections, and was not a ruling of my worth as a human being.

CHAPTER 4

MY NEED TO GRAVITATE towards my grandparents was not solely dictated by the distress I felt around my mother. It was also a bridge connecting me to my father–if not physically, then at least in spirit. At the time I saw very little of him, as he still lived in Akureyri, which today is about a five-hour drive from Reykjavík. In those days the road between the two was unpaved and filled with potholes, so the drive took at least twice as long. Neither my mother or father owned a car, and flying up north was expensive, hence my visits to him were infrequent.

My father was director of the regional theatre in Akureyri–a town of ten thousand inhabitants that had an amazingly vibrant cultural life. There was an established theatre company there that staged ambitious productions, and these were well attended by the townspeople and folks from surrounding regions. My father's home was a small one-bedroom apartment located on the ground floor of a two-storey house, a short walk from the Akureyri theatre. Though it was far from luxurious, I loved everything about his flat. It was full of stage props, posters and furniture from the theatre, each of which held a story. I slept on a bed in the living room that doubled as a sofa during the day. The theatre was housed in an elegant timber building that had been built at the turn of the 20th century using only hand-held tools, and which was infused with atmosphere.

The theatre company was a small one, and though my father was titled artistic and managing director, he also acted, directed, and was involved in all stages of production. Watching a play come to life during rehearsals, feeling the sense of ease and unity that prevailed, being warmly welcomed by everyone in the company–all gave me a deep and gratifying sense of comfort and belonging.

One morning, just after breakfast, my father informed me that he would have to work that evening, and that I would have a babysitter.

"Who?"

"Elísabet."

He was pulling my leg–that was my mother's name. "Ha, ha," I said.

He grinned. "You don't believe me?"

"She's not here."

"Your mamma is not the only one in Iceland with that name, you know."

The babysitter, it turned out, was also named Elísabet, and she worked in the theatre box office. She arrived just as we were finishing dinner, whipped off her coat in a no-nonsense manner, and greeted me with a smile. She was around 20 years old, slender and lithe, with dark hair that flowed down to her waist. My father had to dash, so Elísabet and I cleaned up after dinner, then she plaited my hair into two French braids. She asked if I wanted her to read me a story before bed, but I said that was okay, I could read my own book. She said that was great, since she had to study for an exam. I went to sleep in my father's bed, while she sat on the sofa that was normally my bed, reading a book and making notes.

The next day my father asked how everything had gone. "Fine," I answered. Had I liked Elísabet? "Sure."

The next time I visited my father, several months later, it became clear that he and Elísabet–who was called Lísa by her friends–were a little more than friends. She was around a lot, and they snuck kisses whenever they thought I wasn't looking. We went on outings together to pick wild berries, and had dinner with her parents at their big house in Akureyri. Lísa was younger than my father by about ten years, but the age difference did not seem to matter. Theirs was a harmonious and seemingly uncomplicated union, and they were a pleasure to be around.

I was at my grandparents' house in Reykjavík when I learned that Lísa and my father had gotten married. They had decided to tie the knot because they were planning to go to Sweden for a year, to study. My grandmother delivered the news in an upbeat "guess what?" manner, yet it seemed to me that she, too, had been a little taken aback. The wedding had been a simple affair performed at the local magistrate's office, followed by a small gathering at Lísa's parents' house.

Walking home later that day I had a knot in my stomach, wondering how my mother would take the news, and if I should be the one to break it to her. She knew about my father's relationship with Lísa, but I was not sure if she knew how serious they had become. Fidgeting uncontrollably, I managed to blurt out the tidings, which she received with an outward show of grace. The next day I took the bus to meet my mother at work, then we went to buy a wedding present, from me. My mother selected a guest book with a sheepskin cover–an essential item in most Icelandic homes at the time–which I wrapped and sent them in the mail.

Beneath my mother's outward equanimity, however, there was a seething anger. Her animosity towards my father began to erupt in small, spiteful bursts. Sometimes I could sense they were coming and braced myself for the onslaught, for they felt like emotional assault. My father was a part of me, I loved him, and was loyal to him. Yet my mother voiced her acrimony as though my allegiance was a given–as though my feelings were automatically an extension of hers. I sensed that my refusal to follow her into the dark chambers of her rage would be construed as disloyalty, and that rage would then be directed at me. This prospect terrified me, for I already knew what my mother's anger could do to a tender heart. Underpinning it all was the notion that, unless I was exactly the way she wanted me to be, she would leave me–and what would happen to me then?

One evening after dinner we were in the kitchen doing the dishes–she was washing, I was drying–and I sensed a tirade about my father coming on. I remember that the overhead light felt intolerably bright as she said she had seen one of his friends from the theatre company that day, and that person had looked right through her, "as though I didn't even exist!" I held a glass in my hand and began to dry it frantically, feeling a pressure inside me that I knew I must contain.

"Did you know they call us Elísabet one and Elísabet two?" my mother asked hotly. I nodded, my heart beginning to race. "You know *why*?" I shook my head, even though I did know. "Which one do you think I am?" Her tone was combative and I felt trapped, afraid I would say the wrong thing. When I said nothing, she turned to me, waiting for an answer.

"One," I said dutifully.

"That's right. *One.* These are the friends he was always out with when we were married. I'll never forget that one time he came home from work and said 'Do you want to go out tonight?' I was so happy. I thought he was going to take me out somewhere. But no. Do you want to know what he said?"

Something dangerous was happening: grief, dread, sorrow and anger were expanding inside of me and threatening to explode.

"He said, 'Great, I'll stay home and babysit,'" she finished without waiting for an answer, as though delivering a punchline, her tone caustic.

"*He's my father!* Stop talking about him like that!" I shouted, startling both her and myself. The words exploded out of me–I hadn't meant to say anything, much less to yell, and was instantly terrified by what I had done. There was a moment of absolute silence. My mother stood there, looking at me in astonishment. I threw aside the dish towel I was holding and bolted to the bathroom–the only place in the apartment that had a lock on the door. Slamming it shut, I slid down to the cold tile floor, my back against the bathtub, trembling with the enormity of what I had done: staged an open revolt against my mother by refusing to side with her in the denunciation of my father.

What would happen now? How long could I stay in this bathroom? If I opened the door, would she grab me? Thrash me? Could I get out of there; could I run to my grandparents' place and take refuge with them?

Minutes passed. Fifteen? Twenty? I did not know.

Finally, there was a knock at the door.

"I'm sorry," I heard my mother say.

I did not respond, but relief flooded through me. She would not send me away.

"Can you forgive me?"

"He's my *father*," I yelled, my voice tight.

"I know," she said with something like resignation. "Open the door."

I got up stiffly and opened it. I could not look at my mother. Even though it was early in the evening I went straight to the bedroom, got undressed, and crawled into bed, pulling my duvet up around my ears.

My mother stopped criticising my father after that. She never mentioned him unless it was absolutely necessary, and I understood that I should not mention him, either.

CHAPTER 5

In late summer 1972, when I was nine years old, my mother announced that she was going to Canada to visit Klara and Jim, and had arranged for me to stay with my grandparents while she was gone.

This was fantastic news. Not only would I get to stay with my grandparents for two blissful weeks, I could also ask my mother to buy me a one-piece bathing suit with a skirt. At school we had swimming lessons twice a week, and two of the popular girls had recently turned up in skirted bathing suits. Those suits were not only highly coveted, but also extremely rare. They had been purchased in the United States, so were virtually unattainable unless you had fathers who were airline pilots, like those girls did.

Now, I knew my geography. The United States was close to Canada. Given the proximity, perhaps my mother would be able to find one of those envied items, and a membership to the exclusive skirted-swimsuit club would be mine.

Time passed in a finger snap and my mother returned bearing The Suit, a cobalt blue affair with two big round cutouts in the sides and the most adorable little pleated white skirt. I ran to the bathroom to try it on, and examined myself from all sides. Dang I looked good! I couldn't wait to strut that baby at the pool.

One evening a few weeks after my mother's return she

suggested we have one of our *kvöldveislur*–our "evening feasts". My mother would give me money to go to a nearby kiosk and buy a soft drink, plus a chocolate confection of some kind, for each of us. We would then sit in the living room and enjoy these together, often while listening to the radio, since we did not own a TV.

When I had returned with the goodies and we were sitting down opposite one another in the living room, my mother casually said: "I think you and I should move to Canada."

I took a sip of my coke through a straw, then glanced up at her. "… What do you mean?"

"You and me, move to Canada."

"For how long?"

"Going there to live."

I understood that she was serious.

"No," I said firmly.

"We can have a far better life there," she said quickly. "Klara and Jim are going to help us."

Are going to help us.

She had already decided this.

"There is a city named Calgary where there are lots of jobs," she went on. "We can start a new life there. We might even be able to have our own farm. Maybe we can get some horses."

My grandparents, seeing how much I loved sitting on their neighbour's horse, had paid for me to have riding lessons the previous summer. It had been the most amazing experience of my life, and I was now in love with horses. I wanted so much to have my own horse, but I also knew it was impossible–they cost a lot of money, and we didn't have that kind of money. Yet here was my mother, saying it *was* possible.

"And you could definitely have a dog. They are not illegal in Canada," she added.

Now she had my attention.

"Really?"

"Yes," she said with a smile. "Even if we don't move to a farm, you can have a dog."

I leaned back in the sofa, thoughts racing through my mind. She was suggesting leaving Iceland–again. I did not want to go. Had never wanted to go. This was where I belonged. My father and Lísa had returned from Sweden now and were living in a small apartment in downtown Reykjavík. What was more, they were expecting a baby. I had my grandparents. My piano lessons. My redcurrant bushes. Friends that I played with in the abandoned shipwreck at the seashore. My mother and I had been back in Iceland for just over two years. My father, who for most of that time had lived somewhere else, was finally close enough for me to see him whenever I wanted. I was free to *be* with the people here, which meant I was also free to *become.* I had everything I wanted, except the thing I wanted most.

A dog.

It was just before midday lunch on a Sunday. In my grandmother's kitchen a rack of lamb was in the oven and its delicious aroma filled the air. The midday meal was the main meal of the day on Sundays. Soon my grandmother, grandfather, uncle B, and I would be sitting around the table, dining on lamb, caramelised potatoes, green peas, red cabbage and gravy. I would be drinking Coca Cola with the meal, which I only got to do on Sundays, and for dessert there would be ice cream.

On any other Sunday I would be happy and carefree, enjoying the pleasure of the meal before heading out to play with my friends. But not today. I felt sick with anxiety, for I had to break the news to the people I loved the most that my mother and I were moving to Canada. I felt despicable, like a traitor–ready to abandon them for the promise of a dog.

I cannot remember how I blurted it out, only the deadweight silence that followed. My grandmother lit a cigarette and asked "When?", the adults glanced at one another, and I knew they had Things to Say that they would not say in front of me.

Three days later my mother came home from work a little later than usual. I was lying on the sofa reading a book, but sat up when she came in. She appeared agitated, bustling to the kitchen, then back into the living room, distracted. Then casually, as if it were an afterthought, she mentioned that she and my father had had lunch together.

I stared at her, speechless. Surely she did not mean the two of them sitting at the same table and conversing like normal people … that kind of *together*?

"Why?" I asked cautiously.

"We met to talk about you. Your father thinks you're going to lose touch with your roots," she said, her mouth curling into a lopsided smirk that I knew denoted scorn. "He offered to take you, but we decided that you should try living in Canada for a year, and if you don't like it you can go and live with him."

I did not know what to say. My fate had been determined over lunch, entirely without my input.

"We have decided to rent out this apartment," my mother went on. "Part of the rent money will be used to pay the mortgage, and the rest will pay for your tickets to come back every summer to visit."

I dropped my eyes to look at the carpet, searching for a pattern in the random white, yellow and grey tufts. Sometimes I saw faces; sometimes animals. But right now I saw only a roiling, incoherent jumble of colours.

My mother turned and went into the kitchen. I continued staring at the floor, feeling as though my insides were slowly evaporating into the air around me, leaving me numb.

CHAPTER 6

Our lives are filled with liminal spaces, those places between what was, and what is yet to be. The early morning moments between sleep and waking; the chrysalis in which the caterpillar becomes a butterfly; pregnancy, when a life has been created, but not yet brought forth.

In the liminal transit hall between my old life and the new, an indistinct voice over a loudspeaker woke me from sleep, toneless and dull. Opening my eyes, I blinked. I was lying across a row of hard seats, my head resting on my scrunched-up jacket next to my mother. I remembered now: we were spending the night in an airport. We had flown with one plane to New York, and another to Montreal … but our bags had only made it halfway. Someone had messed up and they were still in New York. They would arrive in the morning, so we were here, waiting through the night.

Around us were rows of seats, mostly empty. Down the hall, a lonely worker pushed a line of buggies.

"What time is it?" I asked, rubbing my eyes.

"Ten past five," said my mother. She looked exhausted.

"I need to go to the bathroom."

Wearily she got to her feet and gathered our belongings–her purse, a plastic bag with some magazines, a half-eaten sandwich, our jackets. We trudged down the corridor to the bathroom. Inside the cubicle I marvelled at the strangeness of the toilet: the huge bowl filled with a massive amount of water, like a swimming pool for small animals. The toilet seat was not round like I was used to seeing back home, but open at the front, like a wishbone.

When I emerged from the stall my mother was at the mirror, trying to hide the bags under her eyes with concealer. I got soap from the dispenser and carefully washed my hands in the sink, soaping halfway up my forearms, like my mother and Klara had taught me to do when I was travelling. Airports, they said, were filled with germs.

I glanced at myself in the mirror. My face was so white it almost looked green.

My mother looked down at me. “Do you want me to put some makeup on you?”

I nodded my assent, then stood still as she smoothed foundation on my skin, brushed mascara on my eyelashes, dabbed lipstick on my lips, and also some on my cheeks, which she smoothed across my cheekbones in a couple of swift motions.

“There,” she said, surveying her work. “That looks better.”

I turned to look at my reflection. I had a new painted-on face for a new life in the New World. I was ready.

Our bags arrived as promised, and when my mother pushed the buggy out through customs I could see Klara and Jim waiting for us beyond the sliding doors. After a brief hug session Jim went to get the car while my mother and Klara griped about Icelandic Airlines and their incompetence in getting bags to their destinations. Exiting the terminal was like walking into a wall of heat. The air was muggy and the moisture stuck to my skin. I had forgotten how the humidity could be thick–so different from the crisp, invigorating air back home. Immediately fatigue bore down on me. I wanted nothing more than to sleep; to become my dreams.

Before long we were on the highway heading towards Kingston, where Klara and Jim now lived. There was a university there, my mother had told me, where Jim was a professor. I must have surrendered to slumber because the next thing I knew Jim was pulling up in front of a big three-storey house made of bricks. In the front yard was the tallest tree I had ever seen, even taller than the house itself. I turned around slowly, taking in the neighbourhood–the brick houses, small yards, lush vegetation, weathered utility poles, and–oh!–across the street *a dog*, tied to the railing of a white split-level house, staring at me as though it had been expecting me.

Jim carried our bags inside and my mother and Klara followed. Not taking my eyes off the dog, I walked slowly to the end of the driveway. It was a miniature poodle, white with splotches of black, and was now on its feet, wagging its tail like crazy. Looking both ways, I hastened across the street, stopping in front of the dog and extending my hand for it to sniff. It jumped up, and when I bent down it tried to lick my face. I laughed with joy and delight. I had not petted a dog in three years and here was one living *right across the street* from Klara and Jim.

There was a sound, and the front door of the house opened. I stood up abruptly. A man was in the doorway, looking slightly unkempt in a T-shirt and pyjama bottoms.

"Hello," he said.

"Hello," I said.

Then he said something that I didn't understand. Since my mother and I had returned from Cyprus I had forgotten almost all my English.

Just then I heard my mother calling me. I glanced at the man, then dashed back across the street, vowing to visit the dog again at the earliest opportunity.

Three weeks passed before I went back, even though the dog was tied up outside the house for some portion of each day. I was afraid the man would come out and start talking to me again and I did not want to stand there like a mute idiot. But late one afternoon after a thunderstorm I summoned my courage and meandered across the street. The sun created little pockets of steam where it hit the ground, and the air was infused with the fragrance of moist vegetation. I sat on my haunches and the dog jumped up and licked my face, wagging its little stump of a tail like the little Icelandic lambs did when they suckled their mothers.

I was talking quietly to the dog in Icelandic when the front door opened and the man appeared, barefoot and wearing jeans and a t-shirt. He held a cigarette in his hand, and the acrid smell of smoke reached me through the scent of wet foliage. I stood up.

"It's okay," he said, "you can pet her."

I nodded awkwardly.

"I overheard you talking," he continued, leaning back against the railing and taking a pull off his smoke. "What language is that?"

"This is Icelandic. I am from Iceland," I said, cringing at my strong accent.

"Iceland?" He raised his eyebrows. "Where's that? Up near Alaska?"

"It's ... I don't know."

I laughed. He laughed too.

"Her name is Piper," he said, nodding towards the dog.

"Piper," I repeated.

He descended the stairs, flicking his cigarette sideways onto the lawn. "Piper likes company, don't you Pipe? You can come over and sit with her whenever you want. She'd love that."

He untied Piper and she bounded up the stairs ahead of her owner, disappearing inside. I waited for the door to close behind them and then skipped across the street. I could come and see the dog whenever I wanted! Sit with her whenever I wanted! I resolved that soon, if I saw that that nice man again, I would ask if I could take Piper for a walk around the block.

"Sure," said the nice man two days later, "you want to take her now?"

Now? He trusted me to take her *right now*?

I nodded.

He went inside and got a leash, then took Piper off her chain and hooked the leash to her collar. "Here you go," he said, "I'll see you when you get back."

I walked to the corner, then turned to look back. The man was still standing on the steps. He waved. I waved. Then I walked on, my back straight and my gaze high, feeling invincible with a poodle at the end of a leash.

CHAPTER 7

IN CANADA THERE WERE many new things to learn, and much for my mother to arrange. She had started work as a waitress in a restaurant called Aunt Lucy's that was situated on the edge of town, and was also going to school during the day to "upgrade her education". This meant that the school she had gone to in Iceland was not considered up to standard in Canada, and if she wanted to get a better job she had to take some classes. Her ultimate goal was to become a bookkeeper.

She also had to find me a piano. I had shown an aptitude for the instrument, and my piano teacher had taken a special interest in my musical education. Before we left she called my mother and respectfully voiced her opinion that I should be allowed to continue my lessons in Canada. My grandparents echoed the sentiment and my mother had vowed to give me the opportunity to learn. She looked in the classifieds and saw a piano advertised for 100 dollars. It was an upright piano, rickety and out of tune, but adequate to my purposes. Klara knew of a piano instructor, and one day near the end of August my mother and I walked the few blocks to Princess Street, Kingston's main shopping artery, to meet with her. I felt light and breezy next to my mother, who looked very pretty in a light-coloured summer dress and sandals. Her skin was tanned, the sun had bleached her light brown hair almost blonde, and she drew looks of admiration wherever we went. I was proud to be seen with her. She was so busy these days that we rarely got to spend time together, and on this particular afternoon my heart was bursting with love and adoration for her.

The music school was situated in a space above a storefront. The entrance was next to a kebab shop, and opened onto a stairwell that was narrow and dark with worn linoleum on the steps and beige walls that were desperately in need of a coat of paint. The instructor's name was Mrs. Cornell, and she was middle-aged and perspiring, with thin, mousy-brown hair down to her shoulders. The classroom was bare save for a piano, a chair, and a threadbare rug. It smelled vaguely musty. All this could not have been more different from the music school back in Iceland, which was located in an elegant old building with high ceilings and whitewashed walls. As the thought occurred to me I felt an intense longing for home, which I swiftly suppressed.

It was agreed that I would begin my lessons in the second week of September, and my mother and I took our leave of Mrs. Cornell. Heading back up Princess Street we passed a shop that sold handbags and pocketbooks. My mother stopped and glanced at the window display, then went in, saying she needed to buy a new wallet. I followed. At the counter a fawning clerk who was clearly smitten with my mother brought out a slew of different ones to show her. Finally, she settled on a wallet that was elongated and opened like a book. Inside there was a sleeve with a hole in the shape of a heart, behind which you could slip a photograph of someone you loved.

"When you get a boyfriend, you can put his picture in there," I said, beaming at my mother.

My mother's laugh was like the chime of crystal. "No, no," she said, "if anyone's picture goes in there, it will be yours."

The clerk smiled at us both. "What language is that you are speaking?"

My mother explained as I stood basking in the glow of what she had just said: that she would put *my* picture in there; that the heart-shaped slot was reserved for *me.*

Leaving the shop, we strolled back the way we came. When we were almost at Jim and Klara's we passed a small house made of yellow bricks with a FOR SALE sign in a tiny front yard. My mother stopped and eyed the house with a dreamy look. "If I had the money I would buy that house for us," she said.

I was a little taken aback. "I thought we were going to Calgary so we could buy a farm," I said, a frown crinkling my brow.

"Yes, well, we'll have to see where life takes us," she said blithely, setting off again at the same tranquil pace.

I was no expert, but it seemed to me that if we didn't move to Calgary, then we might not move to a farm. If we did not move to a farm, I probably couldn't have a horse. I opened my mouth to say something, but changed my mind–best not to shatter the spell of this glorious afternoon by saying something that would upset my mother.

My piano lessons lasted but half a year. Whereas in Iceland I had loved sitting at the piano and practicing my skills, in Canada I became apathetic. No one was around to praise me like my grandfather had, and Mrs. Cornell–who always had foul breath–was unenthusiastic about my progress. On the whole the magic of creativity had vanished for me, and when I said I did not want to continue my lessons, no one made any objections.

Summer drew to a close, and an event I had been dreading was upon me: the first day of school. I was going into grade five, was barely fluent in English, and knew no one.

My mother came with me on my first day. The school building, located just two blocks from Jim and Klara's, was large and stately and made of bricks that were darkened with age and dirt. We ascended wide steps that led to massive double doors at the front entrance. Out in the schoolyard there was the sound of kids playing and loud voices crying out; inside, all was calm and quiet. The building had a high ceiling, and a corridor with hardwood floors so polished they looked wet. I tried to keep pace with my mother as she walked briskly to the school office to find out where I was supposed to go. Next she led the way up a flight of stairs to my new classroom. A woman of short stature wearing a wide dress and sensible shoes stood looking down at some papers on her desk; coming towards us she introduced herself as Mrs. Madison. She exchanged a few words with my mother, then smiled at me and told me to leave my jacket and lunchbox inside the cloakroom on the right. My mother then gave me a quick hug, and left. I stood behind feeling hideously gawky, wearing a hand-me-down kilt that had belonged to Klara's friend's daughter, a white top, and brown sandals. I was not sure what the cool fashion was in Canada, but I felt reasonably confident that it was not kilts.

"Go ahead and find a seat," said Mrs. Madison absently, though not unkindly.

The desks were all different–some were plain wooden tables with metal legs, others had drawers, still others had a top you could lift up and store things inside. I walked to a desk that looked to be the sturdiest of them all. Someone–more than one person, likely–had carved things into the wood: A+E with a heart around it; JON, filled in with ink; KELLY STINKS.

The bell rang, shrill and loud–then there were excited voices, and the sound of running on the stairs. A moment later kids pushed and jostled into the classroom. One girl stopped just inside the door and stared at me for a split second before being shoved into the cloakroom by the boy behind her. A minute later she was standing in front of my desk with two girls on either side.

"That's my desk," she said, arms crossed in front of her chest. She looked ready for a fight.

"What?" I said.

"My desk. You took my desk."

I blinked. How could it be her desk if this was the first day of school? Had there been some pre-school orientation that I'd missed, where kids laid claim to desks?

"I am very sorry," I said meekly, leaning down to pick up my schoolbag.

"I'm very sorry," one of the girls mimicked, and they all giggled.

I took my bag and looked around, feeling so raw and conspicuous that I wanted to die. There were no desks left, and everyone was staring at me. Frantically I cast around for the teacher, who was nowhere to be seen.

A wadded-up piece of paper landed on my back and I heard a snort and a few snickers.

Mrs. Madison bustled in through the door, *oh thank God.* At her desk she stopped and looked at me in surprise. "Is something wrong?"

I opened my mouth but no sound came out.

"She needs a desk," the leader of the girl posse said.

"Oh. Yes. All right."

Mrs. Madison went into the cloakroom and a moment later shuffled back out holding a table with metal legs that she set down next to a window at the back. She went back in and returned with a wooden chair. I went and sat down as Mrs. Madison returned to her desk and started calling out names. Mine was second on the list.

"Ohldah ... Seegm oonds dottier..." she said in a halting voice and looked at me over her glasses, "did I get that right?"

There was dead silence. All eyes were on me. Oh to vanish through the cracks in the floor right now, right now. My name was horrible; a disgrace. And no, she had not said it right, at least not the way it was supposed to be said, not the way it was said back in Iceland.

I nodded.

"That's an interesting name," she said with affected interest, "does it mean anything in particular?"

I shook my head. I was not going to try and explain in my broken English that my first name meant "wave" on the ocean, and that my last name meant "daughter of Sigmund", because in Icelandic we used patronyms and people took their father's first name and added *-son* or *-dóttir* to it, depending on whether they were a boy or a girl.

"Okay."

I released my breath as she moved down the list, calling out impossibly perfect names like Heather and Cindy and Robert and Scott, and the family names: Jackson. Cooper. Williams. Delaney. Oh, what I wouldn't give for such a name. Daughter of Sigmund ... what an abomination!

The rest of day passed like a seething nightmare from which it was impossible to wake up. The teacher talked so fast that I hardly understood anything. The kids stared at me, whispered and pointed, laughed amongst themselves. I wanted nothing more than to escape from there, to go far, far away. To go *home.*

"How was your first day at school?" Klara called as I kicked off my shoes in the foyer. She was in the kitchen, mixing batter in a bowl, a greased muffin tray on the counter next to her. Billy was at the kitchen table, practicing writing in a notebook with evident concentration. I dropped heavily into the chair next to him, crossed my arms and stared straight ahead.

"Was everything all right?"

I shook my head, then leaned down quickly and put my forehead on my arms.

"What is it?" Klara said, mildly alarmed.

"It was horrible! I didn't understand anything. I picked the wrong desk and these girls came and told me to leave. Then there were no more desks and somebody threw a bunched-up piece of paper at me. And when the teacher said my name everybody laughed. I hate my name! I don't want to hear it, ever again. I'm going to change it."

"You can't just change your name, it ..."

"Mamma changed her name!"

It was true. My mother no longer used her Icelandic name. Everyone here called her Elizabeth, and she called herself that when she introduced herself.

"Yes, but that's her first name. The last name ..."

I wasn't listening. "I don't want to go to school here. I don't even understand what the teacher is saying!"

She looked hard at me for a moment, then said: "You *really* can't understand, or are you just saying that?"

"I can't! I can't understand anything. I'm *not* going back!"

"We'll see. We'll figure something out. Don't worry." And she patted my shoulder reassuringly.

The next morning, Klara, my mother and I went to see the school principal–a tall man with skinny limbs and strands of hair combed over a bald head. They sat on chairs in front of his big wooden desk while I stood like a good soldier next to them. Klara did most of the talking, explaining that I had just recently moved to Canada and had a problem with comprehension in the classroom. I did not understand everything she said, but caught the gist. The principal frowned, nodded, and asked a few questions. After ten minutes or so we all got up and filed out of the office.

"Where are we going?" I whispered to my mother in Icelandic as we marched along the hallway after the principal.

"You're going into another class, grade four."

I stopped in my tracks. "Grade *four*? With *younger* kids!?"

"Come on!" she urged under her breath.

The principal came to a door, knocked once, then opened it and gestured for the teacher to come out. She was young and blonde, and had on a stylish skirt and jacket and frosted pink lipstick. The principal talked fast, gesturing towards me. The teacher listened and nodded, then turned to me.

"Hello Alda, I'm Miss Dawson," she said. "Would you like to join us in this class, for now?"

She seemed kind, and my insides flooded with relief. I nodded.

"Good," she said, touching my shoulder and giving a slight nod to my mother and the others. She guided me inside and I found myself in front of another class, curious eyes upon me. I immediately felt more at ease than the previous day. These kids seemed inquisitive, but not hostile. Miss Dawson walked me over to an empty desk next to a girl with long, dark hair in a braid. "This is Vanessa," she said to me, speaking slowly. "Vanessa, this is Alda. She's new, like you, only she doesn't speak very much English. Vanessa is from Australia," she said to me. I sat down gingerly. Vanessa gave me the once-over, then smiled. I smiled back.

"Why doesn't she speak English?" asked a boy with olive skin who sat across the aisle from me.

"She doesn't speak English, Jeremy, because she's new in Canada," said the teacher.

"Where's she from?" he asked.

"Alda, would you like to tell us where you're from?" asked Miss Dawson.

I took a deep breath. "I come from Iceland."

"Where's that?" asked another boy, who was Asian.

"Iceland is a country in the north. Isn't that right, Alda?"

"Yes." I said, clearly.

Miss Dawson walked to the side wall and pulled down a map of the world. "Iceland is all the way up …" she seemed to be searching, "… *here*," she said triumphantly, pointing to it.

The class was silent as everyone gazed earnestly at the map.

"Can you tell us a little bit about your country?" continued Miss Dawson. "Is it cold there?"

I shook my head. "Not too much. A little bit. It's more hot here."

A Black girl in a yellow dress raised her hand. "Do they have polar bears in Iceland Miss Dawson?"

"Hm. That is a very good question Shannon. Polar bears do live in the north." She turned to me. "Maybe you can answer that question, Alda. Are there polar bears in Iceland?"

I was starting to feel uneasy. I did not like being the centre of attention, and was afraid that Miss Dawson would ask me a question that I could not answer. I shook my head. "No. There is … only one polar bear. In a … garden … animal garden …" I stopped. There it was: I didn't know the word. In Icelandic it was "animal garden" but I could tell by Shannon's puzzled expression that this was not the right word in English.

"Do you mean a zoo?" asked Miss Dawson.

Zoo. Was that it? I nodded, hoping it was. Miss Dawson smiled, and the rest of the children seemed satisfied. I exhaled, hoping they would now move on to something else.

No such luck. "She has an accent," the Asian boy observed.

I glanced at him and then at the teacher. *Accent.* What the hell was that?

"Yes. That's normal. Lots of people have accents. Vanessa has an accent too, don't you Vanessa?"

Vanessa looked confused, but nodded.

I made a mental note to ask my mother or Klara what "accent" meant when I got home.

"It's when you talk differently from everyone else," said my mother that evening, when I asked her.

Oh! That was not what I wanted. I vowed to rid myself of this "accent" problem as soon as I could–to tune my ear to the way everyone else talked in Canada. The very last thing I wanted was to be different. I needed to be like everyone else, for only that way would I ever belong.

CHAPTER 8

ALMOST EVERY DAY AFTER school I took Piper for a walk. I had got to know her owners better–the man's name was Kevin, and his wife was Erin. Kevin worked at the bakery where they made Hostess cakes, and got up really early in the morning to go to work. He finished around noon, at which time he went home and slept. Erin worked in an office and did not come home until five–or later if she had to get groceries on the way. That meant Piper was all alone for most of the day, so it was great for her to have me take her for a walk in the afternoons.

Normally Erin and Kevin just left their side door unlocked so that I could go in by myself and fetch Piper. When I returned, Kevin would usually be getting up, and would be very grateful to me for having taken Piper out so he didn't have to do it.

One Sunday afternoon when I brought Piper back, Kevin and Erin invited me to come in for a snack. Erin's niece Leslie, who was around my age, was visiting them. We ate Hostess cakes, drank Kool-Aid and watched TV. I loved the shows in Canada, especially I Dream of Jeannie and The Brady Bunch, but I hardly ever got to watch them because Klara and Jim didn't own a TV. In their opinion TV made you dumb–people should read books, instead.

On this particular Sunday all five of us sat and watched a movie called Planet of the Apes on Erin and Kevin's big colour TV–Piper with her head in my lap. It was hands-down the best afternoon I'd spent in Canada–I felt warm and loved and included, like we were all family. When I left, Erin and Kevin told me that I could come any time I wanted to watch TV, even in the afternoons after I finished walking Piper, when The Brady Bunch was on. I could use the TV downstairs in the recreation room, so that I wouldn't disturb Kevin's nap. My heart was flooded with joy, and I skipped happily across the street when I left, my head filled with musings on what it would be like to be Erin and Kevin's daughter, to have all the Hostess cakes I wanted, and–best of all–to have Piper as my dog.

Those days I saw little of my mother. When I got home from school she was usually at school herself, and from there she went directly to her job at the restaurant, not returning until after I had gone to bed. That, coupled with the fact that broaching difficult subjects with my mother made me deeply nervous, had prevented me from asking her when I could have the dog she had promised me.

But that evening she was not working. After I had brushed my teeth and got into my pyjamas, I tiptoed into her room. She was sitting on her bed, reading.

"Mamma ..."

She glanced up. "Hm?"

"When can we get a dog?"

I watched her face closely for signs of anger or annoyance. "Not until we move," she said.

"When is that going to be?"

"I'm not sure."

"Why can't we get one now?"

"If you hadn't noticed, this isn't our place," she snapped. "And anyway, Billy is allergic to dogs."

I must have looked as stricken as I felt because she added, a little more gently: "I'll tell you what: work hard, get back up to your normal grade in school, and then we'll talk about it."

The next day, after I had walked Piper, I lingered for a long time at Kevin and Erin's, watching TV and doing my homework. I didn't want to leave. I was still there when Erin came home, and came up from the rec room just as she was entering the kitchen.

"Hi!" she said brightly, placing a brown grocery bag on the kitchen counter. "This is a surprise. Have you been here all afternoon?"

I nodded.

"Has Piper been a good girl today?"

"She's been really good."

Kevin entered the kitchen, looking dishevelled and running his fingers through his hair.

"Oh hi, honey," said Erin, "I picked up some ground beef for spaghetti. Did you manage to get some sleep?"

"Yeah, I did. Feel like a million bucks. Can't you tell?" He pointed a finger at me in mock surprise, "Hey, you still here?"

"No," I said.

We both grinned. "Well, do you want to stay for dinner?" he said, looking from me to Erin, who lifted her eyebrows, shrugged and nodded.

"Can I?"

"Sure, if your mom says yes," said Erin. "Why don't you run over and ask her?"

"My mom's at school," I said.

"Well maybe you can ask your aunt."

I pulled on my boots, threw on my jacket and rushed out the door.

Klara seemed a little surprised, but she gave her permission after I assured her that I had not *asked* to stay for dinner–they had invited me.

It was a fantastic evening. Erin made spaghetti and garlic bread, Kevin told funny jokes at the table, and we all laughed. I stayed right up to my bedtime, and as I lay in bed that evening, I fantasised about how Erin and Kevin might offer to adopt me, and how I would say yes–then I would finally be fully incorporated into their family unit, with my beloved Piper by my side.

Time marched on, and soon it was Christmas. Jim and Klara held to the Icelandic tradition of celebrating on Christmas Eve. We had a big dinner, and afterwards all sat next to the tree to open our presents. I was especially thrilled with my present from Jim and Klara: a double album of Donny Osmond's greatest hits. Donny Osmond was my biggest crush–I had his picture tacked up on my wall with blu-tack, and routinely wrote him letters in broken English that I subsequently tore up.

Christmas Day arrived, clear and bright. I wanted nothing more than to go to Erin and Kevin's, but my mother said it would be impolite, at least until late afternoon. Around 4 p.m. I slipped out of the house and ran across the street. I knew Erin and Kevin wouldn't be mad, and I was right, for Erin greeted me at the door with a hug: "Alda! Merry Christmas. We were hoping we would see you today."

Piper turned in circles around me as Erin led the way into the living room where Kevin was sitting, drinking beer with the TV on. She bent down and picked up a package from beneath their tree. "Open it," she said with an expectant smile. I looked at her, feeling mortified–I had not gotten them anything. "Oh that's OK, honey," she said when I mentioned it, "we weren't expecting anything from you. Anyway, that present is from Piper. You give us so much already, every time you take her out for a walk."

I knelt on the floor to open my present as Erin and Kevin looked on. It was wrapped in gleaming white paper with a big red bow. Inside were a hat and scarf with matching mittens, pink and white and very soft.

"Do you like them?" Erin said.

"Yes!" I cried, elated.

"Try them on."

I went into the foyer and put on the hat in front of the mirror, then wrapped the scarf around my neck while Erin watched. "You look so pretty, honey!" she said, giving me a squeeze. I beamed. I was the luckiest girl alive to have them in my life.

New Year's Eve came a week later, and Jim and Klara were hosting a party for a handful of friends. Sara, who was five, came running up to my room in the early afternoon, utterly beside herself with excitement: "Papa bought some sparklers!"

"Some what?"

"Sparklers! Papa bought sparklers!"

Sparklers. In Iceland you could buy as many firecrackers as you wanted–big firecrackers, not Mickey Mouse *sparklers*–in the lead-up to New Year's Eve. At midnight the whole country went outside and set off their bounty, turning the sky into a booming kaleidoscope of colour while everyone whooped and shouted. *That* was a proper New Year's Eve. Sparklers, pfft.

We had dinner, and then Jim and Klara's friends arrived. I went upstairs with Billy and Sara, and Billy and I played Yahtzee while Sara dressed and undressed her Barbie dolls. It wasn't until around ten-thirty that a tipsy Klara came up and told the two of them it was their bedtime. I had been waiting for this moment. All evening the light had shone invitingly from Erin and Kevin's windows, and when Klara and Billy and Sara went into the bathroom to brush their teeth, I used the opportunity to slip out the front door and run across the street.

Kevin opened the door when I rang the bell. He had a drink in one hand and a paper hat on his head. "Heyyyy!" he exclaimed. "C'mon in!"

Piper came rushing into the foyer. Inside I heard people laughing. They had company. I hesitated. "Can I watch TV with Pipe?"

"Sure you can! You don't have to ask, you know that." He looked a little unsteady on his feet.

I took off my boots and lined them up next to the wall, casting a glance in his direction. He did not say anything, just stood there, watching me and grinning. I headed downstairs into the rec room with Piper at my heels and flicked on the TV. The Tonight Show was on, but they kept cutting to some place with big flashing billboards. I turned the dial until I found a movie that seemed promising: vampires skulking around a rundown house; heavy, atmospheric music. It was obviously a movie that had originally been in a different language, but now the characters were speaking English so the sounds didn't match the movements of their lips.

I curled up on the sofa next to Piper, and put my hand on her back. I could feel the warmth of her body through my clothes. Would I love my own dog more than Pipe, I wondered? Was that even possible?

I heard footsteps on the stairs and Erin poked her head around the doorframe. "Hey!" she exclaimed, "do you want anything?"

I smiled happily at her. "No, I'm OK."

She went upstairs and came back down with a bowl of chips and a glass of coke with ice. "Here," she said, "you can't watch TV on New Year's Eve without snacks, it's not allowed."

I laughed and thanked her as I dug into the chips.

I don't know how much time passed before I heard footsteps on the stairs again. This time it was Kevin. He reeled a bit. "Hey," he said, "it's almost midnight!"

I nodded. The movie was really getting good, and I didn't feel like conversing.

"What are you watching?" he asked.

"A movie about vampires," I said.

He sat down heavily on the couch next to me, putting one leg up on the coffee table and taking a gulp of his drink.

"Their talking doesn't match the sound," he said after a minute.

"They're speaking a different language but someone has put English over it."

"Dubbing. It's called dubbing."

"Dubbing."

"They don't do that where you come from?"

I shook my head. "No."

"You don't get films in other languages?"

I wished he would stop talking. "Yes, but we have words at the bottom."

"Ah. Subtitles."

"Yes."

More minutes passed. Then Kevin got up, but instead of going back upstairs like I expected he would, he closed the door. I glanced at him, perplexed. But then I realised–Erin and the others were being really rowdy up there, and he probably wanted to watch the film in peace.

He sat back down, a little closer to me this time. We watched the TV screen. Then, apropos of nothing, he asked, “Have you ever seen a man naked?”

I froze.

“Have you?” he repeated softly.

I mumbled something incoherent.

“I’d like to show you sometime,” he said.

Thoughts raced through my brain. I had to get myself out of there. I knew what this was–images of the tutor at the daycare flashed through my mind. My limbs were petrified and I could not will them into motion. I thought of all the times I’d been alone in the house with Kevin. Had he really been sleeping upstairs? Or had he been lying there, waiting for me to come in so he could show me his ... *thing*?

Then–*oh thank god thank god*–there were voices on the stairs. The spell broke, and I leapt up like a coiled spring. A moment later Erin burst into the room.

“There you are! It’s almost midnight! Come upstairs!”

Kevin jumped up and left the room without even a glance at me. I stayed where I was, perfectly still, listening to Erin stumble up the stairs, followed by Kevin. The moment I heard them on the upper floor I crept into the hall and up the stairs, fearful that if Kevin knew I was trying to leave he would come back. In the foyer I stuffed my feet into my boots, grabbed my coat, and quickly let myself out.

Outside I heard merry voices counting down: five ... four ... three ... two ....

HAPPY NEW YEAR!

⁂

Waking up the next day I had a sick, gummy feeling in my gut. Right away I remembered what Kevin had said to me. I also registered what this meant. It meant that pretending to have a place in Erin and Kevin's family was over. Walks with Piper were over. I would no longer be incorporated into their fold.

It was all finished.

I do not recall feeling much of anything as this understanding came upon me. I only knew that I had to get away, to keep myself safe.

Then, with a sudden sinking feeling, I realised that my Donny Osmond double album was still downstairs in the rec room at Erin and Kevin's.

I had to get it.

I waited until the early afternoon, fidgety and anxious, eager to get this awful task done, wishing I didn't have to. At around 1.30 p.m. I rang the bell to Erin and Kevin's front door. No one answered. I turned to leave, then heard it open behind me. Kevin stood there, wearing only a pair of jeans. He looked a mess.

I stepped into the foyer, my heart racing. "Listen," he said in a low voice, closing the door behind me and glancing down the hall towards their bedroom where Erin was probably sleeping, "I'm sorry about last night. I was a bit drunk."

"It's okay," I replied. My voice sounded weak, and I hated myself for it.

"We'll just keep it between us, eh, Alda? If you don't tell your mother, I won't tell Erin."

As though we were in this together. As though we were both guilty.

I nodded, eyes downcast. He touched my shoulder, and I flinched. Slipping past him, I hurried downstairs. Piper followed at my heels, no doubt hoping I would take her for a walk.

I wanted a chance to say goodbye, so I turned on the TV, hoping Kevin wouldn't come down. I put my arms around Piper's neck and kissed the top of her curly head, stroked her, spoke softly. I told her I loved her and would never forget her. Then I picked up my Donny Osmond album from the floor where I had left it. There was no sound from upstairs–Kevin had probably gone back to bed. I crept up the stairs and slipped out the door, closing it quietly behind me while Piper watched me, her head cocked in guileless astonishment.

CHAPTER 9

THAT JANUARY, MY MOTHER and I moved out of Jim and Klara's house and into our own small apartment. We did not go far–our new digs were exactly two blocks away, in the opposite direction from the school, and consisted of two rooms, plus a kitchen and bathroom, in a house owned by Klara's friend Gillian–the friend who had handed down the kilt from her daughter–and her husband. They had gone away for a year, and offered to rent the downstairs of their house to my mother. The two rooms that were now our bedrooms had originally been a living and dining room, but a partition was put up to divide them. My mother took the front room that faced the street, and I got the one with a view of the backyard.

Yet that was not the only significant milestone that month. I was also reinstated in grade five. My English language and comprehension skills had improved to such a degree that it was no longer necessary to keep me with the younger kids. I had worked hard for this–done my homework each night and made sure I understood everything, read books in English, applied myself consistently and with a clear focus. Just like my mother had said I should do, if I wanted a dog. Now that Billy and his allergies were no longer standing in the way, and I had done her bidding as far as school went, there was no excuse any more for her not to make good on her promise.

"I didn't say you could have a dog," said my mother when I broached the subject, "I said we would talk about it."

"But …"

"We still don't know where we're going to end up, do we? We'll have to move before the year is up, and what if we move to a place that won't allow dogs?"

What about the farm? I wanted to ask, but didn't dare. It was a controversial subject, one that made my mother tetchy. Neither did I want to point out the obvious: that we could simply find a place that *did* allow dogs. My mother had all the answers, and it was hard to argue with her impeccable logic.

One weekend afternoon around three months later I came home and heard low laughter from the kitchen. Shuffling in there I found my mother with a man, sitting at the kitchen table and drinking tea. I stopped abruptly.

"Alda," my mother said, "this is Richard."

I knew my mother had gone on a date with someone a couple of weeks earlier, and guessed this was him. Richard had very short black hair, a bushy black moustache, and glasses with thick black rims. His skin was taut with a waxy sheen, and he had long fingers that he laced together as he rested his hands on the table in front of him.

"Hello, Alda," he said, smiling amiably.

"I was just telling Richard how well you've been doing in school," my mother said. Her voice sounded both proud and strangely formal.

"That is very impressive, Alda, given that you've only been in Canada for a few months. Congratulations!" Richard said smoothly. I could not fail to notice that he had an accent.

Something about this scene set me on edge. I muttered a thank you, then went into my bedroom. A few minutes later I heard them by the front door, talking softly. Then I heard them kiss goodbye.

Richard soon became a frequent guest. First he stayed for dinner, then he stayed the night. In the mornings I could hear him and my mother on the other side of the partition, murmuring and laughing. My mother told me that he was originally from England and had come to Kingston to be a professor at the Royal Military College, which was situated in town. Richard was separated from his wife, but they still lived in the same house with their four children. My mother had been to dinner there, and the wife knew all about her and Richard's relationship, but she didn't care because she had a lover of her own. Richard's wife was a bitch, said my mother. "You should have heard how she talked to him! So mean—so emasculating." I did not know what that last word meant, but I gathered it was bad. "He does not deserve that. That man is so broken."

I listened, feeling just as bad for Richard as my mother did. How awful that this woman should treat him that way. But hey, her loss—our gain. I was delighted to have him enter our lives. Richard had won me over completely two weeks after that first meeting in the kitchen, when he offered to drive me to the Frontenac Mall to get my ears pierced. In grade five all the girls had pierced ears, and if I wanted to fit in–which I most certainly did–I had to have mine pierced, too. My friend Judy, who was in the same class as me, had had hers done just before Christmas, at a place in the mall. This, apparently, was where everyone went. The only problem was that it was on the outskirts of town, and no buses ran out there. You had to have a car, which my mother and I did not. But Richard did, and when he understood how important it was for me to be like all the other girls, he offered to drive me. My mother, Richard and I all packed into his car for an outing at the mall, where my earlobes were duly shot through with a piercing gun. By the time we got back home I loved Richard–or at the very least was deeply grateful to him for his kindness and attention, which in my mind was pretty much the same thing.

My affection for Richard was sealed a few days later when he came to our house with a packet of Wrigley's spearmint gum that he expressly gave to me to thank me for the dinner I had made for him and my mother the previous evening. Judy and I had been allowed to experiment in the kitchen, and had whipped up a tuna casserole with noodles using a simple recipe we had been given in home ec class. As he handed me the gum Richard kissed the top of my head, and I felt perfectly giddy. As far as I was concerned Richard was welcome to be my new father in this new world.

Time passed both slowly and fast. Spring came, school let out, and then it was time for me to travel back to Iceland. It was a strange notion, and I did not know how to feel about it. The previous year had changed me … or, more accurately, had numbed me. My emotional attachment to my people in Iceland had become muted as my loyalties shifted to the only person who was constant in my life: my mother.

I travelled alone from Toronto to Iceland, with a layover in New

York City–a momentous feat for an eleven-year-old. An airport staffer came to meet me at the Air Canada terminal, and we took a limousine to where I boarded the Icelandic Airlines plane. Apart from these details I have little recollection of the trip, except that all went well and I was safely delivered to my father in Iceland.

A few days after I arrived my grandparents gave me a generous sum of money and told me to go downtown and buy myself some new clothes. I was stunned by their generosity. Uncle B's girlfriend Selma took me into town and we threaded the trendy shops, looking for new duds. It turned out to be more challenging than I thought. Before I left for Canada I had known exactly what I liked, and what suited me. Now, I could only stare blankly at the racks of amazing clothes that were so much more stylish than anything in Canada. I was entirely unable to make up my mind about what I wanted, or to envision myself wearing any of them. Today I understand: how we dress is such an integral part of our identity, and I had no sense of who I was any more. Moreover, I did not feel that I deserved to have all those beautiful and expensive clothes. I have since learned that my grandparents gave me the money–not only that year, but also the subsequent two summers–because they were mildly shocked to see the state of my wardrobe, which was both worn and shabby. I, meanwhile, had grown so accustomed to my sub-standard duds that I could not reconcile who I was with these gorgeous items of clothing hanging on the racks of those trendy Icelandic shops.

The six weeks I spent in Iceland that summer were a delight. Everyone was so happy to see me: my father, Lísa, my grandparents, uncle B … even my little sister Jana, who had been only a month old when my mother and I had left for Canada. She was now a cherubic little baby who was just learning to crawl, and whom I found adorable–if, at times, a tad annoying. Knowing how much I had loved my riding lessons two summers previously, my father enrolled me in a week-long riding camp out in the countryside, which I absolutely relished. When that was finished my father and Lísa rented a cabin, where my grandparents joined us and uncle B and Selma came and spent a couple of days. We went swimming, explored the nearby waterfalls and hidden hollows, and spent hours playing Gin Rummy.

The agreement made between my parents–that I could choose whether or not to return to Iceland to live–was not spoken of. I was glad, for the topic made me anxious. I felt that in remaining with my mother I was in some strange way letting my father and grandparents down, yet I also knew at some level that there was no way I could leave my mother.

When I returned to Canada in August I found my mother and Richard busily making plans to move in together. Things had escalated fast. Richard's wife had demanded he move out, and since my mother and I only had our apartment for a few more months, she and Richard had decided it made sense to get a place together. They had an apartment lined up not far from where his ex lived with their kids, which meant I would have to change schools. The upside was that I'd be attending the same school as Richard's daughter Celeste. I liked Celeste, who was sweet and even-tempered, and with whom I got along well. At least I would know one person in my new school, and with any luck we would wind up in the same class.

Moving day was easy since my mother and I had few belongings. Richard supplied all the furniture for the new apartment: a wooden kitchen table with four chairs, painted green; two worn armchairs that didn't match; an old black-and-white TV with rabbit ears that got only one channel. My room had a bed procured from God-knew-where, a plastic bedside table that was actually garden furniture, and a kidney-shaped vanity with a three-way mirror that had previously belonged to Richard's ex-wife. Why he had taken her vanity with him was a source of some perplexity to me, but I did not ask because, well, Richard had changed. He seemed distracted and tense all the time now. When we had lived in Gillian's place he had been kind and generous, but about a month after we moved into the new apartment he did something that seemed really out of character–at least the character I thought he possessed.

My mother was at work at the restaurant, and I was in my room reading, when I heard him call my name in a sharp voice. Startled, I jumped from my bed and went to see what was wrong. He was standing by the front door pointing at my shoes, which I had kicked off and left askew when I came in.

"I would like you to line your shoes up neatly when you take them off," he said.

Glancing at him, a little frightened by his brusqueness, I obediently placed my shoes next to each other and up against the wall.

"Please make sure you do that in the future," he said drily and turned away.

I went back to my room and this time closed the door, careful not to make a sound.

Two days later my mother and Richard and I were sitting at the green table eating dinner. We were having Spam–a fatty processed meat that came in a can. Richard liked to eat it with something called pickled chutney that tasted unspeakably awful. On this day I had no appetite for the Spam nor the wilted salad being served with it. However, I had been summoned and knew I would have to sit there until everyone had finished eating before asking permission to be excused from the table, for those were Richard's rules. I pushed my food around on the plate a bit, then leaned my elbow on the table and cupped my head in my palm.

"Elbows off the table," Richard said in a commanding tone.

I sat up straight.

"Something wrong with your food, Alda?" he enquired.

"I'm not hungry," I said.

"Maybe if you had not eaten before dinner you would have an appetite now," he said. He had this way of speaking words that sounded hostile in a tone that was almost kind.

It was true: I'd eaten a bowl of corn flakes when I came home from school. Richard did not approve of eating outside of regular mealtimes. I stared down at my plate, not daring to look up. The atmosphere around the table had suddenly become very strained.

"I'll finish for her," my mother said, then turned to me. "You can go to your room."

I got up immediately and skedaddled to my room, closing the door and throwing myself on the bed.

I was beginning to hate Richard.

The more I got to know him, the stranger it seemed that he should have such nice children–Celeste, her older sister Monique, and two younger sons, Daniel and Cory. Celeste and I hung out almost every day after school, always at her place. Celeste's mother was French-Canadian, and while she was not exactly warm–that did not seem to be her nature–she was not the bitch my mother had made her out to be, either. At least she was always kind to me. In her house there were very different rules than at our place: Celeste could get things out of the fridge to eat if she was hungry, and everything was fairly laid-back. They had a den with a big colour TV, and when I stayed overnight–which was not infrequently–she and I and the boys piled in there in the morning to watch cartoons.

Meanwhile, at my mother and Richard's flat, everything was very regimented and quiet–eerily so. There was just the old TV with the rabbit ears and the single channel, which my mother and Richard never used because they preferred reading. Richard had strict rules, like the decree not to eat between meals. He also concerned himself with the language we used, insisting for instance that my mother and I not use the word "supper" because in England "supper" meant a light meal you ate late in the evening. I thought about informing him that we were, in fact, not in England but in Canada, where the word "supper" was synonymous with "dinner". But I opted against it, because Richard frightened me. Instead, I marvelled at the fact that a man who thought only lowly people used the word "supper" served Spam out of a can for his precious English "dinnah".

The apartment building where we lived did not allow dogs. This information was imparted via a prominent sign in the lobby: NO DOGS. What did people have against dogs? Why did they have to ban them from buildings, and even entire cities, like Reykjavík?

I mused on this and decided there was no point in asking my mother about the dog. I knew what she'd say. Also, she'd been so annoyed the last time I had broached it that just thinking about it made me nervous.

One Saturday morning, when we had been living in the apartment with Richard for nearly a year, my mother asked if I wanted to join them for a drive. We climbed into Richard's station wagon–banana-yellow with faux wood panelling that he prided himself on having got at a discount due to the garish colour–and drove out of town. We passed the Frontenac Mall, then a building that looked like a fairy-tale castle but was actually a prison, and soon we were on an unpaved road in what looked like a new housing development, that I later found out was called Bayridge. Richard pulled up in front of a split-level house with a yellow brick exterior and a green front door that sat on a corner lot. A woman in a pantsuit and high heels greeted my mother and Richard on the front step, and we went inside. There was a small entryway with a closet, and a staircase leading both to the upper level, and down to the basement. We headed upstairs first. To the left were two bedrooms and a bathroom, to the right a living and dining room, straight ahead a kitchen. From the kitchen a back staircase led down to the lower floor, which was as yet unfinished–wooden posts stood primed for siding, and there was a bare concrete floor and walls made of cinder blocks. The woman explained that one side was meant to be a laundry room, the other a recreation room. Then she led us through another doorway to a part of the basement that was finished. In that section there was a bedroom and a bathroom, and also a door that led to the garage. On the floor there was a thin indoor-outdoor carpet that was an unsightly yellow-brown colour. A staircase led up to the first landing by the front door, completing a circle of the house.

In the car on the way home I laid my head against the side and gazed through the window. My mother and Richard did not say much, but I could tell that they were considering making an offer on the house. I did not know how to feel about that. It was not Calgary. It was not a farm. But it was also not an apartment building that did not allow dogs. If we lived in our own detached house, I reasoned, my mother would no longer have any excuse.

Sure enough, my mother and Richard made their offer, and it was accepted. The house had been a model home and we were thus able to move in a little over a month later. My bedroom furniture–the bed, plastic bedside table and Richard's ex's vanity–were deposited into the downstairs bedroom, which was fantastic because it meant I had the downstairs bathroom all to myself. The green table and chairs went into the kitchen, the clunker of a TV into the unfinished rec room, and my piano, which had not been played for over a year, was fetched from Jim and Klara's and also placed in the rec room. My mother and Richard's bedroom furniture went into an upstairs bedroom, but the mismatched armchairs did not make the cut ... instead my mother and Richard purchased a brand-new sofa ensemble that was delivered late one afternoon about three weeks after we moved in. It consisted of a three-seater sofa–white with a navy blue floral print–a matching armchair, and an ottoman.

I watched with interest as the delivery men carried everything upstairs and Richard directed where it should be placed. When they had left I took a seat in the armchair and put my feet on the ottoman. The armchair rocked a bit, and was exceedingly comfortable. I gave an audible sigh of pleasure.

Richard, who had been deliberating with my mother on the placement of a dining ensemble they planned to buy, stopped talking in mid-sentence and turned to me. "Of course that will be my chair," he said, in that not-unkind voice of his.

I glanced at him and then at my mother. She was staring at him.

"Your chair?" she said with a faint smile, shaking her head slightly. "What do you mean?"

"The master's chair," Richard said matter-of-factly. "I have always liked the idea of having my own chair."

"You mean … a chair that only you can use?" asked my mother.

"Yes, that is what I mean," he said.

I looked from one to the other. My mother looked flabbergasted; Richard mildly annoyed.

I got up from the chair and forced my way through the heavy atmosphere down to my room. I was seething with anger. Richard was such a goddamn asshole; I despised him.

A week later a delivery truck arrived with another chair, this one tall and straight-backed like a throne, covered in gold velour.

"This one's mine," my mother said to me in Icelandic. We always spoke Icelandic when we did not want Richard to know what we were saying. It bothered him immensely. "You can sit in it, too," she added.

I said nothing, but silently I vowed to never sit in either of those chairs.

As the weeks turned into months, my mother and I became more intimately acquainted with Richard's rulebook. It was scrupulous, exact, and extended to every aspect of the household.

One of his pet distractions was the heating. He kept a fierce eye on the thermostat, insisting that it be kept at 60°F if no one was home, but might be turned up to 65°F if someone was home–but under no circumstances must it go higher. The thermostat was situated in the warmest part of the house, next to the kitchen. My room was downstairs in the basement, and that part of the house had virtually no insulation. This was not a problem in the summer, but became intolerable in the brutal cold of the Ontario winter. Each night I crawled shivering under my feather duvet, wearing pyjamas, a wool sweater, thick wool socks, and sometimes even my sheepskin gloves.

Richard had rigid rules when it came to showering and bathing, and kept our water consumption under strict surveillance. Baths were allowed if we filled the bottom of the tub *only*–filling the whole tub, or even half the tub, was forbidden, because it constituted a waste of energy, and therefore money. The rules for showers were equally stringent: the plug had to be left in for the duration to allow water to gather at the bottom of the tub. On finishing, the water had to be left *in* the tub until it turned cold so that its heat could seep into the house and was not wasted. Only short showers were allowed, and the water had to be turned off while I shampooed my hair. I had long, thick tresses at this time, so I was forced to stand and lather furiously and with chattering teeth in that deep-freezer of a bathroom, until I was all clean and could feel the blessed relief of the warm water once more.

I had chores to do around the house, and these included washing the dishes after dinner. One evening, just as I had finished and was rinsing the dish soap from the sponge I had used, Richard came up behind me.

"What are you doing?"

He could not have sounded more incredulous if he had caught me eating the thing.

I spun around. "Rinsing the sponge."

"Rinsing the dishwashing liquid *out* of the sponge," he clarified.

I looked down at my hands. "Okay," I said.

"And why are you doing that?"

"Because, um ...." Was I on a quiz show and was this the million-dollar question? "Because ... it makes the sponge cleaner?"

"No." *Eeehhh'nt*–wrong answer! "You leave it *in* the sponge and use it the next time you do the dishes."

He turned and left the room.

A week later my mother was making tea. I sat at the kitchen table and watched as she put the tea bag into a mug, poured some hot water over it, swished the bag around, then removed it and threw it into the trash bin. Just then, Richard entered.

"What's this?" he said, his voice betraying great astonishment.

My mother glanced up, alarmed. "What?"

"Did you use that for only one cup?"

She nodded, and I thought I saw her swallow.

"Each tea bag is designed to be used for two cups. No need to throw it away. Put it on a saucer and leave it to dry so you can use it again."

My mother pressed her lips together, but said nothing.

Richard, it appeared, was obsessed with saving money. A few days after my mother's great teabag transgression they came home from grocery shopping bearing five cartons of soap. A quick calculation put that at 50 bars. I didn't even have to ask: the soap had been on sale. If anything was discounted, even by just a couple of cents, Richard always bought several cases. The hollow space under the stairs in the rec room had become a repository for canned goods that Richard had discovered on special.

To my bewilderment my mother opened a carton and proceeded to unwrap each individual bar of soap before placing it back in the box.

"What are you doing?" I asked.

"Unwrapping the soap," she said, too busy to even look up.

"Why?"

"So it will dry out and become harder, and won't go all mushy when you use it. That way it also lasts longer."

"Is that what Richard says?"

"Sure. And it makes sense," she said.

To my mother, it did not seem to matter how outlandish Richard's rules were as long as they made sense. That seemed to be her barometer for everything. If it could be rationalised in any way then it was okay, irrespective of how crazy it seemed.

To my mind, things were making *less* sense every day. I had long given up hoping for any kindness or affection from Richard. I seemed to grievously irritate him. Though I did not endorse his innumerable mandates like my mother appeared to, I nevertheless followed them. My sense of normal was getting all screwed up, and in my muddled emotional state I barely noticed. Myriad convoluted, messed-up feelings accumulated inside of me, and I began to think, not that there was something seriously wrong with them, but that there was something seriously wrong with *me.*

When my mother and Richard and I moved out to Bayridge there were still some two months left of the school year and it made scant sense to start at the local school with so little time left. I therefore stayed at my old school, but I could not go straight home from school since there was no public transport out to Bayridge. Usually

I went home with Celeste and Richard would come pick me up after he finished work at the Military College. We then fetched my mother, who had started working as a bookkeeper at a car dealership, and all of us drove home.

I had joined the school choir earlier that year, which now worked out splendidly since I had choir practice after school twice a week. This helped kill the time, and meant I did not have to burden Celeste with my company every single day. The choir was conducted by my homeroom teacher, Mrs. Hayward. As the end of the school year drew near, the choir had begun to rehearse for a final concert that I very much looked forward to.

The evening before the concert, Mrs. Hayward scheduled an extra rehearsal to fine-tune our programme. Most of the children had no issue getting to the rehearsal since they lived close by–but of course that was not the case with me. When I told my mother that I had to attend an evening rehearsal, I watched her tense up. I knew why: she would have to ask Richard to drive me, or, alternatively, ask to borrow his car. I was downstairs when I heard her asking, her voice meek. Richard sounded irked, inquired whether it was really necessary, and cited the cost of the gas needed to drive the ten minutes into town. My mother withdrew from the discussion, then came downstairs and told me that I would have to miss the rehearsal.

I still recall the hopelessness I felt at this announcement. I loved singing in that choir, and the rehearsal was very important to me–yet without Richard's cooperation, I couldn't go, and Richard had made it clear that he would not help me get there.

The next day I approached Mrs. Hayward after class. Downcast, I told her that I would have to miss the rehearsal. I felt ashamed to convey this information, as though Richard's refusal constituted a valuation of my worth, which was lower than the few bucks required for the gas to get me into town.

To my astonishment, Mrs. Hayward asked where I lived. When

I told her Bayridge, she thought for a moment, then told me she would come and pick me up. I was rendered speechless. I knew where Mrs. Hayward lived, and that this detour would add at least half an hour to her own trip–not to mention add to the cost of the petrol, which I had become conditioned to think of at every turn. I could hardly believe that this woman, who was no relation to me and had little vested interest in me attending the rehearsal, was offering to do this, and wanted nothing in return.

Mrs. Hayward and her husband fetched me as she had said they would, and also drove me home after the rehearsal. I recall sitting in the back of their car, feeling very small, as they kept up a casual, easygoing conversation with me, like this was the most natural thing in the world. In hindsight, I wonder if my teacher realised that something was not okay at home, and wanted to extend this act of kindness. Whatever her motive, I am sure she had no idea how much the gesture meant to me, or how it helped to stave off the encroaching desperation I was beginning to feel on a daily basis.

CHAPTER 10

SUMMER CAME AROUND AGAIN, and I embarked on my annual trip to Iceland. My father, concerned that I had lost touch with all my friends there, had introduced me to a girl who was starring in a commercial he was directing that summer. She, in turn, introduced me to a boy she was dating and his group of friends, all of whom were older than me. Consequently, at the tender age of 12 I learned not only to smoke cigarettes but also to drink alcohol–likely not what my father had in mind when he sought this company on my behalf. This, coupled with the new duds I had bought courtesy of my grandparents, had me feeling both chichi and very grown-up by the time I returned to Canada to start school.

I showed up on the first day of grade seven with a carefully-crafted no-fucks-given attitude. I was getting to be an old hand at this–three new schools in three years had taught me that feigning absolute confidence on my first day was key. I now spoke English almost without an accent, which made everything easier–yet there was still the pesky problem of my name. Sitting down for roll call, yet another homeroom teacher began stuttering his way through my impossible name: "Ohlda Zeegm ... oonds ..."

This had to change.

"It's Sigmunds."

"I beg your pardon?"

"It's Alda Sigmunds."

"It says here ..."

"I know. I've shortened it."

He looked puzzled, then shrugged and continued with the names. I glanced at the girl sitting next to me, who grinned. I grinned back.

She was new, like me. Her name was Anne and she was all legs and arms, with a long, pale face and straight blonde hair that hung halfway down her back. She lived near me, and soon we were walking the fifteen minutes to and from school together, every day.

"I'll call you after dinner," Anne said one afternoon when we had been walking the walk for three or four weeks and were about to part. I flinched inwardly. I knew that's what girls did when they were good friends–they continued their daily conversations over the phone in the evenings. There was always more to say. All the girls in our class who were best friends talked to each other like that. Some even had their own phone lines in their rooms so they wouldn't hold up their parents' lines with their endless chitchat.

"Better not," I said, "we …um …"

"Okay," Anne said quickly, surprised and maybe a little hurt.

"We have a party line," I blurted out, reticent and a little ashamed.

"A what?"

"A party line."

She laughed. "*Party* line? Sounds like fun."

"It's not," I said.

She frowned, seeing I was serious. "What the hell is a party line?"

"It's like … we share our phone line with another family."

Her jaw dropped. "No way!"

"Way. It's Richard. He won't pay for a normal phone line."

"What do you mean *share it*?"

"We have the same phone line as some other family. Sometimes I go to make a call and somebody else is on the line, talking."

"So you can listen to what they say?"

"Yeah. And they can listen to what I say."

"Do you know them? Like, know who they are?"

"Nope."

"So ..." I could tell Anne was struggling with this, " ... so, when the phone rings, does it ring at their house, too?"

"No, only at our house."

"But if they pick up the phone while you're talking they can hear you."

"Right. And if we're talking on the phone then the line is busy at their house, as well as at our house. No one can call them if we're talking on the phone, and no one can call us if they're talking on the phone."

Anne was staring at me like I was an alien explaining the rules of my world to her. "That's the most fucked-up thing I've ever heard."

I was relieved to hear her say that. It certainly *felt* fucked up, and I was grateful to Anne for the reality check. Richard got super agitated if I stayed on the phone for more than a couple of minutes because someone might be trying to call the party line people. "Just make your plans with your friend and hang up," he ordered irritably the first time I spoke to someone for more than ten minutes, "you don't need to talk all evening". Clearly he didn't understand the meaning of talking on the phone to a teenager. It wasn't about *plans.* It was about life itself.

"How much does he save with it?" Anne asked, still aghast.

"About half the normal price, I guess."

"Jeez. Is he really that poor?"

"I don't think so. I think he's just cheap."

We were standing in front of my house, around which my mother and Richard had erected a white picket fence, much to my mortification. It was the only picket fence in the subdivision, and probably in the whole city of Kingston. I hated that picket fence–not only was it painfully uncool, it also smacked of a false idyll that absolutely did not exist within the walls of our home.

"Wanna come in?" I asked Anne hesitantly. I wanted her to–wanted her as a friend, but I was also ashamed of my house, which was not like other people's houses. For one thing there was no place for me in it, save for my room that was freezing cold and had cheap-ass furniture. We didn't have a proper TV that I could invite my friends to watch with me, just that old black-and-white job in the bare, unfinished rec room–or should I say "wreck" room, since everything that belonged nowhere else was dumped in there. If I wanted to watch TV I had to sit on a collapsible lawn chair and squint at the snowy reception provided by the two rabbit's ears.

"Is *he* there?" Anne asked.

"No, they're at work."

"In that case, sure," she said cheerfully. "Got anything to eat?"

The two times I'd been to Anne's house after school we'd had our choice of tasty snacks. The first time there was a Betty Crocker cake sitting on the counter and potato chips in the cupboard. The second time Anne's mother had made us grilled cheese sandwiches that we devoured while watching The Price is Right on TV. Anne's house was warm–I stole a glance at her thermostat and saw that it was set to 75°F, even though no one had been home all day. If Anne got cold she simply turned up the heat without bothering to ask anyone, and did not get flak for doing so. Her rec room not only had proper siding on the walls and a shag carpet on the floor, but also a big colour TV with cable, and a ping-pong table. Anne's parents didn't hoard food, they just bought it when they needed it, and did not stick to the cheapest brands only. I was pretty sure this was how normal people did things. In our house, nothing was ever purchased that Richard deemed frivolous. No snacks, no cakes–nothing of that sort.

"I can make mud pies," I ventured.

"What's that?" Anne said.

Mud pies were a concoction I'd come up with. I melted some butter in a saucepan, added sugar, cocoa, oatmeal and shredded coconut, then dropped spoonfuls on a baking sheet and let them stiffen. Then I ate them all, making sure I left no trace so Richard wouldn't know I'd been eating between meals. The mud pies were a particularly good snack because they contained ingredients that hardly anyone ever missed.

"Mm. These are tasty," Anne said as we sat at the green wooden table scarfing down my mud pies and licking our fingers. I grinned, feeling pleased. Yes. Yes, they were.

I could not help being both confused and exasperated by my mother's passivity in the face of Richard's growing tyranny. It made no sense. When we lived in Iceland my mother had communicated to me in both overt and covert ways that I should never rely on a man. I remembered sitting on a bus with her just after we had returned from Cyprus and seeing a woman wearing a gorgeous black lamb-skin coat. When she stood up to get off I turned to my mother and whispered that when I was grown up I was going to ask my husband to buy me a coat like that. Tersely she replied that I should not wait for any husband to do so–I should earn my own money, buy my own coat. I remember how startled I was at this remark, yet how much sense it made to me. Of course I should earn my own money–duh. I began to observe my mother's interactions with men and saw that she was very independent. She dated a few but did not get serious with anyone. One man, Danni, who was around 20 years her senior and owned a flashy car, had wanted her to move in with him, but she refused. Instead, she had moved to Canada.

Then came Richard, and at first she seemed smitten. She had even placed his picture in the heart slot of her wallet–the one she said was reserved for me. It hurt a little that she should give that place in her heart away, but I got it. After all, Richard was all warm and affectionate at first; I had been taken in by him, too. But then she had grown more and more submissive, or so it seemed to me. Now she seemed in thrall to Richard's obsessive control, skulking around and scared to speak her mind.

Disquieting as this was, I confess that the dynamics it created were not altogether unwelcome. In not standing up to Richard, my mother drew closer to me. At times, when he was especially controlling, it felt like she and I were united against him, bonded together in a strange kind of sisterhood. On such occasions I felt connected to my mother at a deep emotional level, such as I had not experienced before. Dimly I realised that, back in Iceland, she had proposed that sort of intimacy when she invited me to join forces against my father–an invitation I had vehemently rejected. Now, however, I was more than willing to join her in a quiet revolt against Richard, and to bask in the sensation of being wronged.

❦

The first semester at my new school passed with relative ease. I made friends with some of the popular girls, and further strengthened my relationship with Anne, who had become my bestie.

On a day in mid-March, Anne and I strolled home from school talking about the latest intrigues. We had stayed to chat with some kids after school and thus reached my house a little later than usual, yet a glance at my watch showed that we had time for a quick batch of mud pies before the dictator came home.

Nearly an hour later, having eaten our fill and high on a sugar buzz, we spilled into the living room, giggling about nothing.

"I dare you to sit in his chair," Anne said, laughing.

I snorted. "No way!"

"Are you scared? I won't tell."

"No! I just don't want anything to do with him. I'll never sit in his chair, ugh!"

"Hey, let's see those dresses he bought your mother."

A couple of months earlier, Richard's father in England had passed away. Three days later Richard was on a plane over there, and stayed for a week. When he returned he brought a whole bunch of clothes for my mother that he had purchased at Marks & Spencer because their clothes were cheap. This included two polyester dresses–the same style but in different colours; two pairs of high-heeled leather boots; and some lacy underwear that he called "knickers". He and my mother disappeared into their bedroom so she could try these items on. She came out a few minutes later wearing one of the dresses, which was maxi-length and had a slit up each side. The fabric was a sort of psychedelic circular pattern, white and purple, and the dress had no sleeves and small buttons halfway down the bodice. I thought it was hideous, but Richard looked admiringly at my mother.

"It fits perfectly," she said, twisting to look at herself in the bathroom mirror, seemingly delighted.

Surprisingly, Richard had not forgotten me. From his suitcase he procured two items for the downstairs bathroom: a plastic olive-green nailbrush and a matching spiky soap holder, to keep my soap from going soggy.

About five weeks later, Richard's mother passed away. Once again Richard went to England and stayed for a week. That time, however, he brought no presents when he returned.

Naturally I had told Anne about the sad passing of Richard's parents and the attire he had sourced for my mother.

Now Anne and I were standing in front of my mother and Richard's closet while I rifled through her clothes, looking for the dresses. Anne, on the other hand, was more interested in Richard's side.

"What the hell is this?"

She was gazing at a long row of pants–pants spanning years–hung neatly on hangers and sorted by colour. She pulled out an especially ghastly pair with a rose paisley pattern on a beige background, made of polyester. "God, are these for real?!"

"You think that's bad? Check these out!" I got out another pair, lime green, also polyester, with a cuff on the bottom. They were way too short for Richard but he wore them anyway.

"You can't be serious."

"And then there's the belt collection," I said, opening another door with a flourish to reveal dozens of belts, hanging in neat order, also sorted according to colour.

By this time Anne was giggling uncontrollably. She took the pants she was holding and started putting them on over her own. I howled with laughter. So distracted were we that we barely heard the car pull up outside. I glanced out the window just in time to see my mother and Richard getting out.

"*Shit!* Get those off, they're home!"

Anne yanked off the pants, jumping on one leg, almost toppling over. Panicked, yet unable to stifle my laughter, I helped her tear them off and snap them back on the hanger. Turning back to the window, I was relieved to see them busying themselves with the hatch of the car. Glancing out again, I spotted something.

Wait. What the …? *Was it* …?

A dog, a German Shepherd, leapt from the back of the car and onto the gravel driveway.

Everything went still. Then the world rushed back in with noise and colour and light.

It was a dog

She had done it!

She had come through for me!

It was not a puppy, as I would have wished, but neither was he fully grown. My mother had him on a leash and was leading him towards the garage–probably wanting it to be a surprise. She couldn't know that I was watching from the window.

I ran from the room, hopped down the flight of stairs, and flung open the front door.

"Hey!" I said, beaming. "What's this?"

"Oh! Hello!" my mother said with a smile.

There was something about her eyes–a furtive look.

Richard sidled up to her and took the dog's leash. The proprietary way he held it stopped me. I blinked in disbelief as my brain struggled to compute what I knew, what I could already see.

That dog was not for me.

Anne came up behind me. My mother and Richard pulled up the garage door and ushered the dog inside. Turning quickly, I went into the house, pulled on my boots, and grabbed my jacket from the closet. Anne didn't ask, just did as I did. I rushed to the sidewalk and half-ran down the street. I had no plan. I just needed to keep walking, away from there … away from them.

"What happened?" Anne asked, alarmed, catching up to me.

I told her the whole story. How my mother had promised that

if I came to Canada with her I could have a dog. How it was never possible–there was always some reason for why she couldn't fulfil her promise. And now they'd brought home that dog, and it was not for me, but for *him.*

"Are you sure it's not for you?"

I shook my head. "It's not for me."

"Maybe it's supposed to be for both of you," she said reassuringly. "You don't know that."

"I do," I said. I knew Richard would never agree to share a dog with me. Not in a million years.

"Maybe she'll get one for you, too," Anne pressed. She was doing her best to make me feel better.

I shook my head. "She won't," I said.

We were in front of her house by now and sat down on the front step. A torrent of thoughts and feelings raged inside me.

"What are you going to do?" Anne asked after a bit.

I just shook my head again.

"Do you want me to ask if you can stay for dinner?"

"No thanks."

I couldn't tell her that I didn't want to stay for dinner because I wanted to stay *forever.* I wanted her life. Her parents. Normal, kind, *good* parents. Who wanted to see me happy. Who kept their promises, didn't care if I had a snack after school, or whether I put my shoes in a perfect line. I wanted a home where I could gossip with my friends on the phone, and take a long, hot bath if I felt like it.

Richard named his dog Chappy and kept him in the garage. He did not want him in the house because he didn't believe in spoiling dogs.

One afternoon after school, a few days after my mother and Richard brought Chappy home, I carefully opened the door that led from the house to the garage. I wanted to see Chappy; wanted to go to him, pet him, talk to him. He was chained in the furthest end of the garage with an army blanket to lie on and some food and water in two bowls. He stared at me. I stared at him. He did not wag his tail.

I took a step towards him. His tail went up, as did the heckles on his back. He bared his teeth.

"It's OK, boy," I said.

He growled.

I turned and went back inside, closing the door softly behind me.

Richard took Chappy for walks after work on a short leash. He was teaching him to heel. Chappy pulled on the leash, and Richard got impatient, yanking him back. I watched from the upstairs window, then went downstairs.

I didn't care. I did *not* care.

Chappy barked at people. He lunged, too. I overheard Richard telling my mother this in a somewhat accusatory tone, like it was her fault that Chappy behaved this way.

Chappy lived for another five months. That August, while I was away in Iceland, Richard took Chappy to the vet, where he–Chappy, that is–attacked the vet's assistant. Richard subsequently made a decision to have him euthanised, and so ended Chappy's sad, chained-up life.

CHAPTER 11

THAT SUMMER, MY FATHER and I toured Iceland together while Lísa and Jana visited Lísa's parents in Akureyri. We went to see a friend of his who was restoring an old house on an island called Flatey, then went to visit my uncle H who was working as a chef at a hotel in the West Fjords. It was a wonderful, easy, joyful time. Back in Reykjavík, as my departure for Canada drew near, I began to feel a mounting anxiety–a sense of dread that I could not connect to anything in particular. I only knew that I did not want to leave.

One evening, when Lísa was putting Jana to bed, I went to my father, who was cleaning up the kitchen after dinner.

"Pabbi," I said hesitantly.

He turned around. "Hey. What is it?"

"I … can I still come and live with you?"

He stopped wiping the counter, and turned to face me.

"Why?" he said. "Did something happen?"

I shook my head. "No," I said. "No, not really. I just like being here. I want to stay."

He motioned for me to sit down, then sat opposite me. "You know," he began, "it's one thing to visit here in the summer, and another to live here permanently. When you come in the summer I have a lot of free time, and we can do fun things. I don't have that sort of time in the winter. It's very different."

"I know," I said, feeling a leaden weight settle over me.

"Your mother would be so upset if you didn't go back."

I nodded. He was right. I shouldn't even have brought it up.

"Maybe we can get your ticket changed so that you can stay a bit longer–until school starts," he said. "How about that?"

"Okay," I said.

"We'll call your mother tomorrow and ask if it's all right."

I nodded.

My mother was taken aback when I called, and I immediately felt guilty. She asked to speak to my father and after a bit of wrangling, she agreed. I had an extra three weeks of bliss, and then flew back to the place that, like it or not, was now my permanent home.

I went into grade eight, and got through the winter by finding ways to hang out at my friends' homes in the evenings. I made sure I never overstayed my welcome or became annoyingly ingratiating, for fear that I might not be invited over any more. It went without saying that none of my friends were ever invited to my house in the evenings.

I recall two memorable events from that year. One was a Saturday afternoon when Richard took his three youngest kids swimming, and then came back to our house with a box of donuts he had picked up on the way. There was one for each of the kids, one for him, one for my mother, and none for me. When my mother expressed surprise that I had not been included, Richard made some furtive response about not thinking that I would be there. My mother cut her donut in two and gave me half, but I found the whole experience humiliating, as it was probably meant to be.

The other incident was a letter that I received from my father, informing me that he and Lísa were going to separate. I found the letter in the mailbox before I went to school, and read it quickly before I had to rush out the door. A couple of hours later, while working on a problem in math class, I started to feel an odd, unwell sensation that I could not very well define. I asked to go to the bathroom, yet as soon as I was out in the hallway I felt like I was going to collapse. I crouched down in the small alcove outside the classroom where we hung our coats, my back against the wall and my head in my hands. I wanted to cry, to wail, to ... *something*, but I was inert; frozen. A few minutes later a teacher walked by and found me there; concerned, he asked what was wrong, and whether I was sick. I didn't know what to say, so I said nothing, only shook my head back and forth, over and over. He walked me to the school office where a receptionist phoned my mother, and she agreed to let me go home early. I felt a terrible sense of overwhelm, but could not label or identify my emotions. It felt like they were packed inside me like filling in a stuffed toy, inaccessible unless I burst a seam, at which they would all explode out of me, messy and chaotic.

That, I decided, must not happen. The seam would have to hold.

The fact was, of course, that by now my subconscious was filled with so much unresolved junk that I had begun to stagger and trip along the road to maturity. The abandonment of my true self and my alignment with the persona I had subconsciously decided to create–an avatar that went out into the world and interacted with others–became further solidified as I struggled to process the awful emotions that were beginning to build up in me: frustration, anger, panic, doom, and a horrendous sense of being trapped. I had hoped to escape to my father's care, but now even that avenue was closed. And so, I began to look for other escape routes.

In the summer of my fourteenth year, just before starting high school, I was walking along a quiet Bayridge street with three of my friends: Anne, Darlene and Jody. We had been down at a small plaza that the neighbourhood kids dubbed "the store" since it contained the only convenience store in the 'burb. This was our hangout, the place where we met up to horse around, smoke cigarettes, flirt and consider ourselves badass–as teenagers do.

A car with a loud engine and racing stripes drove by, then came to a stop a short distance away. The windows were down and we could hear loud, pumping music. A guy with thick auburn hair and freckles leaned out the window on the passenger side: "Hey, you girls got a light?"

Anne had one. She stepped over and handed him her cigarette, which he used to light one that he had in his mouth. I glanced into the car. The driver was leaning forward and looking through the passenger window, with a wide grin that turned his eyes into narrow slits.

"What are you girls up to?" asked the passenger guy.

"Nothing much," Anne said. "You?"

"We're headed out to a party at the quarry, wanna come?"

We had heard about the clandestine parties at this "quarry" that was out in the boonies around a half-hours' drive away, and where kids sometimes went on sunny days to sunbathe and swim.

We glanced at each other. Anne looked at me and shook her head slightly.

"I don't think so," I said.

"You sure?"

We were sure.

Five days later, on a Friday evening, they showed up again, this time down at the store. We talked for a bit, and learned that the driver's name was Manuel, and the passenger was Steve. As before, they were headed to a party at the quarry, and this time we went along. The four of us piled into the back seat of the car and

Manuel set off, tires squealing, out of the township and onto dim, forested country roads. He drove so fast that the bottom of the car touched the ground when he flew over a rise in the road. Steve yelled "yee-haw" as Anne and Jody laughed nervously. I set my jaw and tightened my grip on the grab handle. I didn't like this–though at the same time, I did. It cut through the deadened parts of me and made me feel alive.

When we got to the quarry, around 50 people were already there, drinking and partying. Someone had turned up a car stereo and was blasting "Paradise by the Dashboard Light" by Meatloaf. There was a bonfire. Manuel and Steve opened the trunk of the car and handed each of us a beer. We moved closer to the fire, and soon a joint came my way. I had never smoked weed, but took a puff and felt it burn my throat. I coughed, then passed it to Anne. Glancing past her I saw Manuel looking at me by the warm glow of the flames.

The music grew louder, the mood more frenzied. Over to the side there was a commotion, and we all turned to look. Some guys were pushing a car–an old Pontiac with its headlights on–towards the edge of the quarry pit. People were shouting, clapping and whooping like this was some bizarre ritual. A moment later the car reached the edge, and with a last push slid vertically into the water, sinking slowly into its depths, its headlights emitting ghostly beams. A few guys yelled and cheered. I couldn't believe what I was seeing; nor could I understand the point of this mind-boggling escapade. Yet there was something in it that resonated with me–some release of primal frustration and anger, a desire for destruction, to tear down convention or the status quo. I felt alarmed, yet at the same time, soothed.

The following week, Manuel showed up at the store by himself. Anne and I were sitting on a low wall when we spied his car. He ambled over to us, grinning like crazy, looking almost embarrassed to be there. I found his awkwardness endearing. He told us that he was from Portugal, had lived in Canada for eleven years, and had come over with his whole family–parents, three brothers, one sister. We asked how old he was: 21. Where he lived: downtown. Where he had gone to high school: Kingston Collegiate, but he had dropped out as soon as he turned sixteen. Did he work? Yes, at his brother's house painting firm.

Manuel became my first boyfriend. He would come and pick me up at the store, or as the weather grew colder, at some pre-arranged location closer to home. We arranged these trysts in advance, since we could not call one another on the phone. In no conceivable universe was I going to introduce Manuel to my mother and Richard, and Manuel had no plans to trot me out to his parents, either. They wanted him to date a nice Portuguese girl, not some Canadian floozy. To Manuel's parents, any girl who lived in Canada, kissed boys, and was not Portuguese, was awarded that title. We'd go out driving, park along deserted country roads, drink beer and smoke weed, and fumble around in each other's clothes. I was fourteen, a virgin, and frightened of Manuel's body and its sexual urgency, but I made sure I did not let it show. I wanted to seem older and more mature because I was afraid he would reject me if he thought of me as a little girl and I needed him to provide an escape route–to help me get out of the house, away from my mother and Richard. He had a car, and he always brought something–usually beer, or weed, or both–to take the edge off. And so, I convinced myself that I was in love with him.

Though Manuel was always kind, the unspoken understanding between us was that he would not stick around unless we took things further in the sexual arena. This scared me. I didn't know what to do, what was expected of me, what grown women did when they had sex with grown men. I fancied myself an adult, yet I was only a child. To buy time I said I wanted to wait until I was fifteen, vowing to myself that I would, in the interim, search the pages of Cosmopolitan magazine for instructions on how to satisfy Manuel.

He agreed to wait, but reluctantly. Under no circumstances would he ever agree to wait for a girl in this way, he told me, though for me he would make an exception because I was a virgin. To Manuel and his friends, "breaking in" a virgin and having her bleed for them was the greatest conquest of all. Through some law of nature, according to them, said virgin would be meekly devoted to her conqueror for the rest of her life. For that reason, and that reason only, he agreed to delay intercourse until my fifteenth birthday. But if at that time, he stressed, he found out that I was *not* a virgin, well then ... and he raised a hand as if to slap someone. Me.

At the time it did not occur to me to question the legitimacy of this virgin blood fixation, or why Manuel should have a "right" to my body–as though my body belonged not to me, but to him. My fifteen-year-old self considered it exceedingly generous for him to wait this long, and I felt guilty for even insisting on it.

As we moved deeper into winter, evening dates on dark country roads began to lose their appeal. In lieu of this Manuel decided to introduce me to two of his older brothers, so we could go visit them in the evenings. Both brothers were married with kids, and neither they nor their wives spoke much English. Or perhaps they opted not to speak it with *me*, for it was evident that both wives considered me suspect. They mostly ignored me as I sat at the dining table with the men, drinking beer and smoking, while they waited on us: whipping up food, bringing beer, removing bottles and cleaning ashtrays.

Manuel had another brother, John, who was a couple of years older than him, and whom he always spoke of with veneration. I had not yet met this John because he was currently incarcerated. The hilarious Story of John was told and re-told: he had been racing down a street in his car, drunk, and failed to notice that the street came to an end. Where the street came to an end there was a house with a bay window. John crashed his car through the bay window and into the house where the owners were watching TV in their jammies. They had the shit scared out of them, but were unhurt, so it was all fine and we could have a jolly laugh about it. John, the renegade, had had his drivers' licence revoked for life because this was not the first time he had been arrested on serious traffic violations. He was serving nine months in jail and would be out very soon, at which time I was assured there would be a big celebration.

This momentous event took place on a cloudless Saturday in late October. With the scent of burning firewood drifting through the air I headed down to the store, where Manuel had arranged to pick me up. I was feeling buoyant–my mother and Richard were going to a dinner party so I didn't have to report home until sometime around midnight. Manuel was waiting in his car when I arrived, and even through the windshield I could see his face lit with excitement. As soon as I got in he exclaimed fervently: "John got out of jail–three weeks early!" Everyone was at his brother Jose's house, he said, so I would get to meet John. We'd go straight there.

It was only noon but already I could smell the liquor on his breath.

Pulling into Jose's driveway I heard laughter and loud voices through the open front door. Entering the house, the first person I saw was John. Indeed, I couldn't *not* see him–he had placed himself squarely at the centre of attention. He was about the same height as Manuel but more muscular, with a bushy moustache and thick wavy hair. Hips thrust forward, he talked loud and fast in Portuguese to a rapturous audience, but when he spotted me and Manuel in the doorway, he stopped. "Aahh...!" he exclaimed taking a step towards us, a lascivious grin on his face, looking at me and then at Manuel ... "aahh-ha-ha...."

"This is Alda. Alda, ..."

"Al-da!" he repeated, coming towards us and looking me up and down. He winked at Manuel. I wanted to puke.

"Hello," I said.

John slapped Manuel lightly with the back of his hand, and there followed an exchange in Portuguese that I didn't understand. Manuel headed to a bucket filled with beer bottles on ice, fetched two, opened them, and handed one to me. I took a seat on one of the couches next to a girl I had never seen before and who I figured was Deb, John's girlfriend. Manuel had told me about her. She, too, was a "Canadian floozy" and lived somewhere near me. She was very thin, with straight, mousy hair and an apathetic manner that suggested she did not seem particularly thrilled to have her man back from prison.

John had taken centre stage again and the story continued. Even the Portuguese wives stood watching, holding their toddlers in their arms, tut-tutting yet smiling in spite of themselves. Manuel came over and squeezed in next to me, putting his hand on my thigh.

"What's he saying?" I whispered.

"He's talking about this guy in jail that he was always fighting with, this Paki ... he put his dick in John's mouth one night when he was snoring, so John shat in his shoe. The Paki got up and put his shoe on and it was full of shit." He guffawed and shook his head in a "whadda guy!" kind of way.

The afternoon passed in a haze. We drank beer, then some more beer, then there were joints being passed around, then a bottle of Southern Comfort. I wasn't sure how long we had been there when Manuel spoke in my ear: "C'mon, we're going."

"Where?"

"For a drive. To see some people John hasn't seen in a while."

I would have preferred to keep vegetating on the sofa, but got up and followed Manuel outside. John was shoving a case of beer into the trunk of the car, and I could see another case in there already. Deb stood dispassionately over to one side, purse over her shoulder, a paper bag in the shape of a bottle in her hand.

"*Let's go, let's go...!*" John shouted, darting around like a disoriented hamster. Manuel bounded down the steps and into the car. John and Deb piled into the back, I got in the front. Manuel revved the engine, punching the gas with his foot, and took off squealing.

We drove aimlessly for around twenty minutes, Manuel turning corners seemingly at random, John and Deb making out in the back, pausing periodically to take swigs from the bottle. Finally, John leaned forward and said something to Manuel in Portuguese. He nodded, turned, and headed out of town.

"Where are we going?" I asked, a little concerned that it might be far and we wouldn't be back in time for my curfew.

"Go-Kart track."

A few minutes later we stopped in front of a yellow hut with a big sign leaning against it that read GO-KARTS. Off to the right there was an oval racetrack with a bunch of little buggies parked near the starting line. Next to the hut stood a flashy white Firebird with wing decals on the hood, spread out like two flames. Out of the hut stepped a guy, maybe thirty, with long blonde hair cut in a shag. He paused on the steps, eyeing us. John walked over to him, while Manuel and I wandered over to look at the buggies. A few minutes later I heard loud voices, and turned. John and the Go-Kart guy appeared to be arguing. Manuel left my side, strode over there and the three of them began an animated discussion. My head was spinning and I thought maybe I should stroll around the track to see if I could sober up a bit. Then I heard a whistle. I glanced over, and saw Manuel motioning for me to come.

He was getting into the back seat of the car when I reached him, and grabbed my arm. "We're gonna have a race," he said.

A quick computation established that Manuel would not be able to drive from the back seat, which meant ....

I went rigid. "I'm not getting in," I shouted in a whisper, glancing in John's direction.

"C'mooon," Manuel droned, "we're only going down the road. Just three minutes. You can close your eyes."

John was heading over now, a cigarette dangling from his mouth. I had a bad, bad feeling–yet still, I climbed in. Manuel put his arm around my shoulders and his hand lightly over my eyes. "Don't be scared," he said in a soothing, fatherly voice. The car jerked into motion, then rumbled slowly out of the parking lot and onto the main road. I heard the door of the Firebird slam and the engine rev. John shouted something unintelligible through the window. Then the white Firebird was beside us on the road. John laughed hysterically, and an instant later I was pushed back in the seat by the velocity of the car taking off, next to Manuel who sat stiffly, his face frozen in his trademark grin.

The rest happened quickly. The car began to skid, and I sensed more than I saw John frantically turning the wheel, struggling to regain control. Then there was a strange feeling of floating, and I had the sensation of being knocked about. As from a distance I heard crashing and the sound of breaking glass; I curled into a ball and put my arms around my head. Then there was stillness, and a sound like a hissing kettle.

There was movement under me and I realised that the car was lying on its side and I was on top of Manuel. He was saying something about crawling out the driver's window that was now above us, as John and Deb had already done. It seemed hopelessly far away. I didn't even know if I could move but it turned out I could; I climbed up and out through the window that had been fully down, thank God, so there were no shards of broken glass to slice into us. My breath came in spurts, my mouth was dry, and I was terrified that the car would tip over when I climbed up. But it didn't; from the window I jumped onto solid ground and a second later Manuel was there, too.

My legs felt weak and wobbly and I sat down hard on the grass. Manuel wandered to the left, then to the right. Deb sat over to one side, puking, blood on her face and in her hair. John was busy near the trunk and it took me a second to realise that he was tossing beer bottles from the car. "Help me get the fucking booze out!" he shouted, sounding furious. But I couldn't do anything, I just sat and looked at Deb and then at the wreckage of the car, then up at the road, and back again. We'd tumbled down an incline lined with boulders that looked to be about twenty feet high. The car had rolled at least once and spun around, so the front was facing back the way we came. The body was bashed in on all sides, and steam came from the engine. The hood had flown open and was twisted like a piece of liquorice. The windshield was smashed.

I heard Manuel and John talking in feverish voices. John was shouting and then shoving Manuel and a second later he had him down on the ground and was sitting on top of him with his fist in the air, apparently ready to hit him in the face. I saw Manuel trying to shield his head and heard him say, "Okay, okay..." and then John let him go. Manuel got up, dusted himself off, came over to me and said, "We're going to tell the cops I was driving, okay?"

"What?" I felt disoriented; he wasn't making any sense.

"When the cops come, tell them that I was driving. Okay? We can't let them find out John was driving. He'll go back to jail. I'll get off. First offence." His voice was clipped, breathless.

Just then I heard the first sirens. They came closer and closer. Within minutes, five police cruisers had arrived, and two ambulances. They screeched to a stop up on the road, red beams flashing. Paramedics clambered down the slope towards us. One came and put a blanket around me, asked if I was all right. I nodded.

He exchanged a glance with a cop.

"We need to take you to the station to give a report," the policeman said. "Can you walk?" I got to my feet. He supported me up the slope, led me to a cruiser, and opened the door for me to get in the back. He got in the front, and noted something down on a clipboard. "You're pretty lucky, you know that?" he said, "If one of those rocks had hit the gas tank, the car could have exploded. You could all have been killed."

I nodded, only half comprehending, and stared out the window. I saw Manuel and John, illuminated by flashing red lights, being led to the cruiser in front. Both had been handcuffed. An officer led Deb to the cruiser I was in, and opened the door for her to get in next to me. She had bandages on her face and the blood had been wiped away, but one of her eyes was beginning to swell.

We were taken to a small police station on the outskirts of town. The place appeared makeshift, like it had been cobbled together in haste. All was quiet. A clock above the reception desk ticked away the minutes; twenty, thirty, forty. Finally, a door opened and one of the constables from the scene stood in the doorway. "Deborah," he said. Deb quickly stubbed out her cigarette and rose, smoothing her pants and walking through the door with a straight back. About a quarter of an hour passed before the same officer appeared and called my name. Nail-bitingly nervous, I followed him to an office where a man in uniform, whom I had not seen before, sat behind a desk.

"Take a seat," said the man behind the desk, gesturing to a chair in front of the desk. I sat. "Alda, is it?" he said, looking at me over the rim of his glasses. I nodded. "I'm Sergeant Paltrow, this is Constable Longman. Now, we understand that you were in the car that went off the road. I'd like to ask you: where were you sitting?"

"In the back," I said without hesitation.

He glanced down at some papers, then back at me.

"We understand that there was a race going on."

"Yes."

"Can you tell us who you were racing?"

"Some guy from the Go-Kart races."

"And you were sitting in the back seat."

"Yes."

"And who was driving the car you were in?"

"Manuel."

"Manuel, your boyfriend, was driving?"

I nodded. "Yes."

There was a pause. Sergeant Paltrow levelled a look at me. "Why were you not sitting in the front seat next to him?"

"I ..." I faltered.

He sat back and looked directly at me. "You should be aware that Constable Longman here is a witness to anything you say. Giving a false statement is a serious offence. There will be a trial, and you may be asked to testify. When you do, you will have to tell the truth. Lying on the stand is even more serious than giving a false statement. Do you understand?"

I lowered my eyes, trying to keep the dread from rushing in. I had promised Manuel that I would tell the cops he was driving, but what if they found out the truth? What would happen if I kept lying and they discovered what had really happened? I might get sent to juvenile prison. Was it worth it? Would Manuel break up with me if I did not do as he said? Yes, he provided an escape from the toxic atmosphere of home, but was I willing to go that far? Was going to prison better than being trapped in a house with *them*?

"I'm going to ask you again: who was driving the car?" said the Sergeant in a measured tone.

I lowered my eyes. "John," I said on an outbreath.

"Pardon?"

"John," I repeated, a little louder.

He leaned back in his chair. I lifted my eyes. He was gazing at me with satisfaction.

"If it makes you feel any better," he said, "your boyfriend has already admitted that his brother was driving."

I exhaled. It did make me feel better. It did. At least Manuel could not accuse me of having ratted him out.

Constable Longman and another officer drove me home. I had not seen Manuel, or John, or Deb after my interview and had no idea where they were. Sergeant Paltrow had said that the officers would have a word with my parents when they brought me home, but to my great relief my mother and Richard were not yet home from the dinner party. Before I got out of the car Sergeant Paltrow reiterated that I might be called on to testify at Manuel and John's trial, and would therefore need to tell my parents. I gave him my solemn promise that I would.

The house was dark when I let myself in. I went straight to my room, stripped off my clothes, put on my pyjamas and washed my face. I got into bed, pulled my duvet up around my neck, inhaling its familiar scent. In Iceland, everyone had their own duvet, starting with a baby one when they were born, and upgrading as needed. Mine had been a gift from my grandparents before I left for Canada, and nothing I owned gave me greater comfort. I tried to sleep, but it was futile. Thoughts raced and spun in my mind like snowflakes in a storm.

An hour or so passed before I heard my mother and Richard come home. They lingered a while in the hallway, then my mother came downstairs. I lay perfectly still. Should I pretend to be asleep, or should I tell her? If so, should I tell her now? She barely knew about Manuel ... only that there was someone I was kind of dating, but no more than that.

The door opened a crack and she peered in, then retreated. I rose up in bed. "Mamma," I said, my voice feeble.

She opened the door again. "I thought you were asleep."

I reached over and turned on the light on my bedside lamp–faux marble plastic, in the shape of a mushroom.

"I need to tell you something."

She came and sat on my bed. She had been drinking; I could smell it on her breath. Sitting with my back against the wall I told her what had happened, leaving out the part about my own drinking, and about John having just got out of jail, and about the lie we told the police. She sat very still and listened. Then she asked me a few more questions about Manuel and how serious our relationship was ("not serious, he's mainly a friend"). Suddenly she leaned over and clutched me to her. I was taken aback; I could probably count the number of times she had embraced me on the fingers of both hands.

Releasing me she said, "Do you have a Bible?"

I looked into her face, perplexed. What a strange thing to say. My mother was not particularly religious, and as far as I remembered we had never talked about God.

"I ... um, I think so." The Gideons had visited my school a couple of years back and given everyone a pocked-sized copy of the New Testament.

"I always find that it helps to read The Bible at times like this," she said.

I got out of bed, and rifled through the drawers in Richard's ex-wife's vanity. I found it there, in the middle drawer, shoved to the very back.

Bidding me good night, my mother went upstairs, leaving me down there with The Gideons. I opened The Book at random. "No, I strike a blow to my body and make it my slave so that after I have preached to others, I myself will not be disqualified for the prize." *Okay.* That made no sense. I was glad my mother had come down to check on me, glad she had not been mad, and glad for the hug. But that invisible, impenetrable barrier that always existed between us was still there, and I did not feel comforted. Turning off the light I burrowed deep under the covers, trying hard to ignore the chasm of emptiness and despair that I knew was in there, growing bigger by the day.

CHAPTER 12

Now that Manuel's car was destroyed it was more difficult for us to meet. The drama of the accident, the impending trial, our forced separation, all injected pain and yearning into our relationship, which I mistook for love. I savoured these emotions, because they made me feel ... something. I had not told my mother about the impending court proceedings, and each day I nervously checked the mailbox before she and Richard could get to it, in case I had received a summons to testify. But three weeks passed and no summons came.

Manuel and I saw each other only once before the trial. A bus service of sorts had been introduced out in the suburb–an old repurposed school bus with hardly any suspension that now stopped at the end of my street. After winding its way through seemingly endless crescents and avenues belonging to three different subdivisions, it ended its route at the Kingston Shopping Centre. This scenic tour of suburbia took a full sixty minutes, whereas a car ride from my house to the same destination took ten. Still, I was happy to put in the time if it meant getting into town without having to beg someone for a ride.

There was a German-style restaurant in the shopping centre where they were not sticklers about ID, and where I, at fourteen, could get served alcohol. About two weeks after the accident, Manuel and I met there over beers to discuss the potential outcome of his trial. One of three things might happen, he said. First, he might be acquitted. In that case he would call me at home at 4 p.m. on the day of the trial, where I should be waiting by the phone. In the second scenario he would be found guilty, but would not begin serving his sentence right away. In that case, same arrangement as before. Third, he would be found guilty and be taken to prison immediately. In that case, obviously, he would not be able to call, so if the phone didn't ring I could assume that he had been incarcerated. I would then call Steve the following day to find out what happened.

At 4 p.m. sharp on the day of the trial I sat at the kitchen table, staring at the phone on the wall, willing it to ring. Anne, who was there for moral support, sat next to me. Five minutes passed. Ten.

"Maybe he forgot," Anne said, chewing on a thumbnail, "give it a few minutes". I nodded, pale with tension.

By four-thirty there was still no call. I felt like my life was ending.

The following day I went home with Anne after school, and called Steve. He gave me the lowdown: Manuel and John had been found guilty and taken directly to Joyceville penitentiary, located about a half-hour's drive northeast of Kingston. Manuel had been given a six-week sentence. John, the repeat offender, had been given nine months.

I stayed at Anne's for as long as I could, then trudged up the street towards home, heartsick and deflated. On opening the door, I heard my mother in the kitchen, and saw Richard in his master's chair, legs crossed, holding up a broadsheet newspaper. I took off my shoes, lined them neatly up against the wall, then padded quietly to the kitchen, hoping Richard wouldn't notice me. No such luck. Lowering the newspaper, he said in a smug, gloating tone: "I see your 'friend' has been sentenced to prison."

I felt the blood drain from my face. Was the outcome of the trial in the newspaper? If it was, how did he know that the Manuel in the paper was *my* Manuel? Ignoring him, I went into the kitchen. My mother stood there, hands on her hips. "So. You didn't mention anything about a trial," she said angrily without preamble, in Icelandic. "And this *Manuel*..." she spat his name, "he is twenty-one years old?"

"How do you know all this?" I asked, my voice weak.

"It's in the paper," she exclaimed, evidently disgusted. "The 'In the Courts' column. And what exactly does 'misleading police' mean? What did he do?"

Standing in the middle of the kitchen I spilled the whole story of John and the driving. I spoke Icelandic, knowing that Richard was sitting on the other side of the wall, craving details to feed his righteous indignation.

"Who *are* these people you've been spending time with?" she asked angrily when I was done.

How to answer? Could I say that I spent time with *these people* because Manuel was my refuge? Because his displacement in Canadian society mirrored my own? Because I had little in common with my peers who had loving families, warm homes, and who were valued for who they were? Because Manuel provided access to substances that helped me stay anaesthetised? No, I could not tell her that, because I didn't know those things yet. All I knew was that I clung to Manuel because he felt like the only person on whom I could depend.

"They're my friends," I said.

"Are you going to keep seeing that guy?"

I shrugged. *Yes* I thought, but didn't say so.

"Well, if you get pregnant, don't expect *me* to raise the child for you," she snapped.

The remark was so unexpected and absurd that I nearly burst into laughter. Manuel and I hadn't even had intercourse yet, and the notion of my mother raising our love child was beyond ludicrous.

"Oh, I won't," I said. Then I turned and went downstairs, vowing that I would wait for Manuel for as long as it took for him to be released.

I waited four weeks. He was let out early on good behaviour and arrived home a few days before Christmas. We resumed our relationship, and that spring Manuel and his pal Steve rented an apartment out in the 'burb, not far from where I lived. I spent long hours there, feeling very grown up–cooking and cleaning, washing dishes in the kitchen, picking up beer bottles from the living room, emptying ashtrays–doing all of the things I had seen the wives of his brothers do. Yet I was starting to grow weary. Manuel's drinking was getting out of hand. His hands trembled like crazy when he had no booze in him. "Your hands are shaking," I'd say, and he'd say, "It's just nerves". He couldn't fool me, though. He needed that bottle like my grandfather had needed it during his "sick" spells.

I was developing an aversion to him–his drinking, his lifestyle, his lack of ambition. By now Manuel and I were having regular sex, yet despite his staunch conviction to the contrary, I had not morphed into a blushing maiden who fell adoringly at his feet in the wake of my deflowering. Quite the opposite, in fact. I wanted to end it with him, but didn't know how. It seemed that the flip side of Manuel's proprietariness was a newfound dependency on me. He constantly told me he loved me and could not live without me, and any time I tried to disentangle myself I was overwhelmed by guilt and a sense of responsibility for his welfare.

I had begun leaning on Manuel because he provided a way for me to escape the emotional wasteland of home. Yet a new option for escape had since presented itself: a roller-skating rink, where we neighbourhood kids could skate to disco music or hang out in a game room stocked with pinball machines and pool tables. This provided a welcome, and rather more wholesome, alternative to hanging out with Manuel and his crowd.

In late summer, about a year after we first got together, I at last found the strength to break up with Manuel. After we parted ways he seemed to disappear, and I heard through the grapevine that he'd gone out West, to the land of opportunities where my mother had originally planned to take us. The next time I saw him I was working as a cashier in a supermarket at the Frontenac Mall, and suddenly he was there, standing next to the till. Only a couple of years had passed, but he looked a decade older. He still had that smile that turned his eyes into slits, but his teeth were tobacco-stained, his skin sallow, his shoulders too hunched for a guy in his mid-twenties. I was too busy serving customers to give him much of my time, but learned that he had recently moved back to Kingston. After a few moments of stilted conversation he walked away with a swagger that belied his insecurities, while I went back to ringing up groceries.

What is it that causes us to choose one path over another? Manuel asked for little more out of life than to stay perpetually numb, and it would have been so easy for me to do the same. I expect we'd both experienced trauma. I knew nothing about his, and he nothing about mine–in fact, we probably had very little awareness of our own traumas at that point, and were incapable of sharing them with anyone, much less each other. Yet Manuel's efforts to escape had him careening headlong into a wall, while I had an unassailable sense that there was something better that awaited me, even if I could not clearly formulate that thought at the time. Somewhere I knew that I had to keep moving towards the light, or I would die.

CHAPTER 13

THAT AUTUMN, IN THE year of tenth grade, my fellow students and I were informed that we would need to choose a vocation for our adult selves, and begin selecting courses that would further us along the road to that destination. I found this requirement impossible, for I could conjure up no vision of a future. My main preoccupation was getting high–sneaking out during breaks to smoke hash or weed in the bushes next to the school. When prompted to say which courses I especially enjoyed, or which subjects I might wish to explore further, I drew a big, fat blank. I didn't particularly like anything. The subject at which I most excelled was typing.

And yet, in those rare hours when I still had an inner dialogue, I occasionally admitted the existence of this one thing. It was not a dream, exactly, but rather a glass bauble so fragile that I barely let myself examine it for fear that it might shatter. It was salvaged from a lost past, a tiny flame that I had managed to keep alive and hidden from anyone who might wish to extinguish it. This tiny thing was a memory of the time I had spent in the theatre–the joy, vitality, and sense of being connected to the creative force. It was, I realised, a time when I had felt most alive.

As the deadline I had to choose my courses drew near, I grew increasingly despondent. I could not acknowledge the flame to anyone, and yet I also knew that if I did not, it would be deprived of oxygen and would die. Finally, I made an appointment with the school guidance counsellor, hoping she might help me. I told her I had no idea what I wanted, and she proposed that I take an aptitude test, to help determine my strengths and proficiencies. I sat in her office and shaded in little circles next to the answers to various questions, and when I was done she instructed me to come back in two days' time for the results.

I showed up at the appointed time, eager to see the verdict, secretly hoping that *the thing of which I dared not speak* would be there at the top. I yearned for that validation, that permission to follow my heart's desire. "I want you to keep in mind that this is only meant as a guide, and that if something is at the top of the list, it doesn't mean you have to pursue that line of work, or even that you should," the guidance counsellor explained. Her words barely registered, so eager was I to see myself defined by the sheet of paper she held in her hand. She handed it to me, and I perused it breathlessly. At the top was not my deepest wish, but a profession I had never even considered: *Writer.* My heart sank. I moved down the list: *Teacher. Journalist.* Finally, at number twelve, there it was: *Actress.*

Number *twelve.*

"Of course there may be professions further down the list that might appeal to you more, and that you might wish to pursue," the counsellor was saying. Had she read my mind?

I swallowed. "I ... there is something I think I might want to do," I said in an unsteady voice.

"And what might that be?" she asked kindly.

"I think ... I might like to do theatre?" My inflection was that of a question–as though I was asking for her permission to follow this profession.

The silence that followed felt like it went on forever. I interpreted it to mean a million things: She considered me delusional; she thought me profoundly untalented; the idea was ludicrous; I was ridiculous; I should give up now; who the hell did I think I was?

"Have you taken part in any school productions?" she asked.

I strained to hear the condescension in her voice, but found none.

"I ... ah," I faltered. The truth was that my music teacher, who also directed the school play, had made a point of speaking to me the previous year, urging me to audition for the lead in Anne of Green Gables. A music test I had done in his class had revealed that I had perfect pitch. I had felt a momentary surge of something warm, an unequivocal happiness, yet at the same time I knew I would not audition. Why, I did not know.

"No," I told the counsellor.

She frowned, and looked down at a sheet of paper that held my grades in the previous year. "I see that your grades were all good last year, except for one class." She looked up at me. "The only class you came close to failing is drama."

I wanted to wilt under her gaze. It was true. I had almost flunked that class because I'd acted like an asshat in it. I'd been flippant and irreverent and the teacher had formed an aversion to me. I totally got that. I had formed an aversion to myself too. Every time I stepped into that classroom I had become a weird version of myself, someone I intensely disliked, who was cool and above-it-all and who wanted to sabotage everything. I couldn't seem to help it.

"My mother doesn't want me to do drama," I said.

The words escaped my lips even before they had taken shape in my mind. I blinked, astonished at myself. I'd had no idea I was going to say that.

"Why not?" the counsellor asked, surprised.

"I don't know."

It was true: I didn't know. We had never talked about it. Not about the theatre, and not about my father. In fact, these days we rarely spoke about anything except the logistics that facilitated our living together under the same roof. It was strange, therefore, that

I should harbour this conviction–that my mother did not want me to do, or be, something. Why did I think that?

"I'd like to call your mother in for a meeting," the counsellor said, eyeing me intently.

Her gaze made me uncomfortable, as did the suggestion that she wanted to talk to my mother about what I had said. Under no circumstances did I want my mother to think I had ratted her out, or bad-mouthed her. My heart rate accelerated. "What for?" I asked.

"Just to talk about your future, and how she might support you."

I considered this. Maybe it would be a good thing–she might have other ideas about what I could do–things of which she might approve.

The meeting was scheduled for the following week. I waited nervously for my mother at the school's front entrance. She arrived on time, wearing a knee-length skirt, a silky blouse, and a pair of the high-heeled boots that Richard had brought back for her from England. She looked elegant and sophisticated, and I felt immensely proud as I walked alongside her through the school, past the communal area, and to the counsellor's office. I knew few people in the school who had a mother as young and pretty as mine.

In the counsellor's office, my mother appeared poised and self-possessed. She smiled, and looked at me with an affection that she rarely showed at home. I felt myself blossom in the warmth of her gaze.

The counsellor opened with a short preamble about the difficulties I was facing in choosing a path for myself. Then she said, "Alda has expressed a wish to work in the theatre–perhaps to be an actress."

My mother looked from her, to me, and back again. "She has?"

I fidgeted in my seat.

"She is concerned that you may not want that for her, though, and that you might not support her," the counsellor went on. My stomach lurched. Why did she have to say *that*? And to say it *like that*? My mother would surely take this as criticism, and be angry.

But she was shaking her head. "Of course I want her to be an actress, if that's what she wants," she said with just a tiny hint of defensiveness. She turned to me. "I'll support you in whatever you want to do, you know that!"

I dropped my eyes. I wanted to apologise, but it didn't seem like the right thing to do.

"Lovely," said the counsellor and smiled.

After some more general talk about my schoolwork and aptitude, we all rose. The meeting was over. I walked my mother out, then went back to my classes. She and I never discussed the meeting again, I never took another drama class at that school, and I never tried out for any of the productions.

Early evening in November, not long after the meeting with the counsellor, I sat at the kitchen table idly reading the newspaper comics and eating a grilled cheese sandwich. I no longer ate dinner with my mother and Richard, partly because I wanted to be out of the house by the time they got around to serving dinner, and partly because I now had a job at a clothing shop in the Frontenac Mall, called The Loft, working two evenings a week, plus Saturdays.

On this particular evening I had plans to meet my friends at the roller rink. My mother came into the kitchen, puttered around at the counter for a bit, then sat down opposite me. I stopped mid-chew and glanced up. She had an odd expression on her face–exhilarated and nervous at the same time.

"What?" I said.

She spoke in Icelandic. "You know how we always planned to get a farm."

I stared at her. Please, I thought, *don't*.

"Well, we've just made an offer on one about an hours' drive north of here. We want to grow our own vegetables and raise our own livestock. And I'm going to make my own cheese."

I stared at her. "Where did you get the money to buy a farm?" was the only thing I could think of to say.

She explained that when Richard's parents died they'd had thousands of pounds in savings. All their lives they'd scrimped like they were destitute, and no one–certainly not Richard or his sister–had expected to find this wealth stashed away in the bank.

"If our offer is accepted we'll try to move next spring. I'll quit my job but Richard will keep working in town, so you can get a ride with him in the mornings and he'll pick you up at the end of the day, just like before."

I was having some trouble computing this. Moving to the boonies, dependent on Richard for rides–the same Richard who had refused to drive me even ten minutes into town for choir practice. Removed from all my friends. An hour's drive away, out in the country, with no means of escape. It had been bad enough being out here in the 'burb. Put me into isolation with the two of them on a farm and I would surely go insane.

"What if I don't want to go?" I said in Icelandic, trying to keep the panic from my voice, hyper-aware of Richard in the next room, listening.

"Don't you want to?" she asked, incredulous. "I thought you wanted to move to a farm."

In that moment I did not think that there might be something extremely *off* in my mother's unequivocal expectation of me to accompany her out to that place, after all that had gone before. In those days, I was unable to see my mother's bizarre behaviour for what it was. All that came later. For now, I was just too busy surviving. There at the kitchen table my thoughts were already racing, madly searching for an escape route. Where could I go? What could I do? How could I live? I was fifteen going on sixteen. Could

I quit school, find a job, rent my own place? What kind of job would I get without even a high school diploma?

"We'll get a horse, and a dog–maybe even two of them," my mother was saying.

I blinked. She was talking but I no longer heard what she was saying. I had to get out of there. I stood, walked around the table, opened the trash, and let the remainder of my sandwich slide off the plate and into it. Richard would be furious when he saw it there, but fuck him.

I took the back stairs down to my room, and lay down on my bed, staring straight up. I felt like the world around me was imploding. What would I do? What would happen to me? I knew I would not go. I *could not* go. How many moves had I made with my mother already? Uprooted time and again, denied the opportunity of long-lasting friendships or relationships–except the one with her, which was fickle, at best. She had always managed to entice me with gilded promises, but I had stopped believing in those. I would not be duped again.

And yet ... neither could I bear the thought of them leaving. Even with Richard's bullying, his control fetish, his incessant monitoring and censure of everything I did; even with his swords on the wall, cannon ball casings on side tables and assorted military paraphernalia as house decoration, even with my mother's meek deference to him, her unreachability, her disregard of me ... I wanted them to stay–for how would I survive without them?

I spent the next few weeks steeped in ceaseless anxiety. The reality laid out before me was grim: I needed money if I was to have a place to live; to get money I would have to work; to work I would have to quit school; if I quit school I would never have a decent job.

I had told my mother that I would not go with them. She had

initially been very dismissive, implying that if that was what I wanted, fine, I could suit myself. Then, probably realising that she might get judged for offloading me so easily and moving on, she came down to my room one evening and asked me to reconsider, saying she wanted to have me with her a little longer. *What for?* I thought–it was not like our relationship was particularly enjoyable for either of us. The bond I had felt with her once, of the two of us being united against Richard, had disintegrated after the incident with Chappy. The distance between us had grown more pronounced and I knew she and Richard talked about me, and bonded over my "difficult" behaviour that, as far as I could see, was mainly down to the way I shunned their company. In this triangle that was the three of us it seemed that, for there to be harmony, either Richard or I had to be "it"–the persona non grata. Either it was my mother and Richard against me, or my mother and I against Richard.

My mother was never "it".

I wrote to my father. Not because I wanted to move back to Iceland–that hope had been quashed–but to ask if the income from my apartment, the one earmarked for my trips back home in the summers, could be made available to me here, now. Before he answered my mother told me that she had written to him and suggested that they each pitch in a monthly sum to help cover the rent of a room or small apartment for me, that would at least allow me to finish high school. I would, however, have to keep working evenings and weekends to cover my food and expenses. The very fact that she was thinking of these things brought me immense relief–even as the prospect of being thrust into adulthood and learning to look after myself, while trying to finish school, continued to cause me great angst. I was racked with worry about this imminent and monumental change to my life, and how I would manage. Deep down I could not shake the feeling that I was being punished for my aloofness towards my mother and Richard, that this was my mother's way of getting back at me for her perceived slight or rejection of her.

Weeks passed in this state of uncertainty. It felt like a slow erosion of my soul, interspersed with bursts of desperation and panic.

And then, one evening, my mother came down to my room, sat on the edge of my bed, and outlined a plan she had devised to deal with the unexpected problem of my wilfulness.

It was not a surefire thing, she said, but her proposal was this: we would sell the apartment in Iceland, and try to get the proceeds from the sale out of the country. Iceland had strict currency restrictions in place, she explained, so we could not just transfer funds across the border at will, but there had recently been some relaxation of the law, and her brother-in-law in Iceland was looking into our options. *If* it was possible, given the high rate of the Icelandic króna against the Canadian dollar, she might be able to buy a house for me in Canada. Best would be to purchase a house downtown, on or near the university campus, where I could live and also rent out rooms to students. The revenues from that would cover the cost of the small mortgage I would have to take out. We could buy a car for me with a part of the proceeds, to make it easier for me to get to school, and also so I could drive out and visit her at the farm. With any luck the sale of the apartment in Iceland would have happened by the time the house in Bayridge was sold, and I would be able move into my very own home.

I listened to her speak with growing amazement. Never in my most outlandish dreams could I have conceived of such an arrangement. Me, with my own house, and my own car? Living alone–not out in the 'burbs, but downtown? With no more Richard to harass me? Abandoned, yes–but also free?

All of a sudden the future began to take shape, and it looked less bleak than it had in a very long time.

CHAPTER 14

THE PLAN WAS SOON put into action.

My uncle in Iceland investigated and discovered that it was feasible to move proceeds from the condominium sale from Iceland to Canada, though it would have to be done in two or three instalments. The apartment in Iceland was put on the market, yet weeks went by and there were no offers.

In the spring my mother and Richard took possession of the farm and gradually began their move. First they started staying there on the weekends; then they started moving stuff. The master's chair was one of the first things to go–it went with the master, naturally. Ditto the gold velour throne, with the mistress. The sofa stayed in the house, until one evening I came home from work and it was gone. Then went the dining ensemble. The stereo. Some pictures. Eventually the place was almost bare save for my bedroom furniture and the kitchen table and chairs.

The house reflected my emotional state: the more cavernous it became, the emptier I felt. This begat a strange paranoia within me, beginning with the niggling sense that someone was watching me from outside, monitoring my every move. The feeling grew more intense when darkness fell, and had me scrambling to close the curtains so that this strange imaginary nemesis could not see inside. Yet there was one pesky window that could not be shuttered or blinded–a small one in the front door, more or less at eye level. That window was like a mocking eye, constantly turned on me–a menacing presence, harsh and condemning, a persecutor I could not escape.

That summer, for the first time since my mother and I moved, I did not fly back to Iceland. There were last-minute complications with my ticket, and making new arrangements within a suitable time frame was not feasible, hence I settled with my father that I would come at Christmas instead. I had no objections to staying in Canada, for I had discovered that living alone in a big empty house lent itself rather well to partying. I could now invite people over to drink and hot-knife chunks of hash and no one cared that I didn't have a decent TV. I had started dating a guy six years my senior who worked at the stereo shop across from The Loft–his name was George and he was dubbed "Gorgeous George" for his dashing good looks. He took me out for dinners and drove me home after work. And so, I did not bemoan my missed trip to Iceland. Instead, I relished being the girl who was home alone, and who moreover had one of the town's most desirable men on her arm.

While my trip to Iceland that year did not go as planned, my mother's strategy for selling the apartment did. One afternoon she called me on the phone and announced that the flat was sold and the first chunk of money would arrive within a month.

This gave us the green light to start looking for a house. "Us" in this case meant my mother and Klara–my involvement was very limited. Soon they found one that they considered suitable–downtown, a few blocks from Jim and Klara's, near the university campus. My mother came into town and the three of us went to view it, my mother and Klara marching through the rooms speaking rapidly in Icelandic, me wandering slowly behind them, my brain in a dense fog. I had smoked a joint earlier and would have preferred to munch out and then fall asleep.

"It's perfect. You can rent this part out to students," said my mother gesturing to the upper floor. "The rental income will cover the mortgage and a good part of your living expenses."

I noted that no mention was made of how I might fly back to Iceland, now that the income from the apartment was no more. My mother had effectively closed the door on Iceland. She had only been back to visit once, briefly, since we had lived in Canada, and had no plans to go anytime soon. She had become a Canadian citizen, and invited me to take citizenship with her, as her child. Yet it would have meant renouncing my Icelandic citizenship–Iceland did not allow dual citizenship at that time–and I could not imagine turning my back on my native land. I had therefore turned down her offer.

"When you graduate from high school, you can apply to Queen's University and live here," my mother was saying. Apparently she considered it a done deal that I would continue to live in Canada, and in Kingston, with her. I nodded automatically, casting around. This place would need a bit of work if I was to live here. The kitchen floor was covered in pink and lime green linoleum tiles, and the walls of the living room were bright pink–almost fuchsia. The bathroom was a study in industrial green: green tub, green sink, green toilet, green walls. The good thing about this house, though, as my mother pointed out, was that there were two kitchens and two bathrooms. With some strategic shutting of doors I could have my own little apartment at the back of the house, with a living room, tiny bedroom, kitchen and bathroom. The back door was my private entrance, separate from the rest of the house.

"Good," my mother said briskly. "I think we'll take it."

❦

And so it came to pass that, at the tender age of seventeen, I owned my own house, drove my own car, wielded my own credit card, balanced my own checkbook, managed my own tenants, and did my own shopping, cooking and laundry–all while getting top grades in school, working three shifts a week at the mall, and staying super skinny. I had migrated within the Frontenac Mall from The Loft to the Dominion Store supermarket, which was a tad less glamorous, but which paid a substantially better hourly wage and offered better shifts. I drove to school each morning in a shiny blue Honda Civic purchased with a part of the sale proceeds, and on the weekends hosted gatherings for my friends before we all headed out to the bars that were now conveniently located within walking distance.

To any outside observer, I was living The Life. I had it all, and held it together seemingly without effort. While most of my girlfriends wallowed in self-doubt and uncertainty about their relationships, body weight, and life in general, I had everything figured out–for myself *and* them. Should they break off that engagement with the boyfriend they'd had since the start of high school? Yes, *obviously*–they needed to play the field before they settled down. Should they tell their parents they didn't want to go to medical school and would prefer to be a hairdresser? *Of course*–it was their life, not their parents', right? Should they take a year off before deciding what to enrol in at university? *Naturally*–why waste time doing something you weren't invested in? I had the right answers for everyone, and I was consistently amazed when people chose not to heed my advice and made stupid choices that I knew would only lead to their unhappiness. Such weakness, such self-sabotage, could only lead to self-pity and martyrdom. Why couldn't they get a grip? Why was it so hard for them to make something of their lives?

I had none of their problems. Everything was grand with me. Granted, I had no relationship drama to deal with–my liaison with George had been terminated when I discovered that he was a compulsive liar. Also, he hated my cat, a grey shorthair named Dexter. Viewing Dex as a rival for my affections, George would grab him by the nape of the neck and throw him into the bathroom if he so much as jumped up on the couch. The final straw came when I screamed at George to leave Dex alone, and he slapped my face because, in his view, I was hysterical. When it came time to decide which one to keep, the choice was easy.

So, yes, I was winning at life. Except … that relentless judge that resided outside every window in the dark was becoming more and more insistent. He demanded nothing short of perfection from me, especially when it came to my body weight. I needed only to step on a scale and discover that I had gained half a pound for him to deliver his verdict that I was worthless and disgusting. To appease him I began to obsessively monitor my calorie intake–from Monday to Friday I stuck to a diet with military precision, eating no more than a thousand calories a day and exercising compulsively. Yet my ironclad resolve crashed and burned on the weekends in spectacular fashion. I would hit the bars, drink myself into a stupor, and then "go out for food" with my girlfriends. This meant gorging myself insensible with whatever was in front of me, then heading to the all-night donut shop for more, stuffing my face like I would never eat again. I spent Saturday loathing myself for my loss of control, yet in the evening the same thing would repeat itself: to the bars, drink, binge. Sunday, hung over and bloated, I would vow to never do it again, and would embark on a purge. That would last for the next five days, and then the whole manic process would begin again. If I exceeded 105 pounds on my 5'5" frame I was filled with revulsion for myself; if I was under that weight, I felt strong and in control. The baggier my pants were, the happier I was.

The fact that my life was spinning out of control was utterly lost on me. I had no grasp on anything, yet clung to the illusion that I did by fiercely controlling my body weight. I thought I was stronger than everybody, yet I was terrified of people, of relationships, of intimacy. Going out to the bars with people was fine–situations where I kept up appearances, yet was in permanent escape mode. If someone dropped by my house without announcing their arrival I flew into a panic, scrambling into the tiny corridor between the kitchen and the living room and hiding there until they left. I presented one side of me to the world, but the private me–the fearful, paranoid, obsessive me–I kept resolutely hidden.

I had shut down all emotional connection to my past, and when you have no past, it is hard to have a future. I had a year left of high school, and beyond that I saw nothing. I was no more prepared for the future than I had been that day in the guidance counsellor's office, three years earlier. No plan and no vision. The only thing I knew was that I would go back to Iceland after graduating, to visit my family. On some level I clung to the hope that this trip would help me gain clarity, that I would find the little girl I had left behind, and that together, she and I would forge a path forward–the path we were always meant to travel.

CHAPTER 15

It was in this no-man's land between an erased past and an obscure future that I first met Shane. I had sworn off relationships, had come to think of them as a pointless hassle and that I was much better off on my own. But when I saw him winding his way through the crowd one evening in a club, holding a tray high above his head, moving with a self-assurance that informed me that he did not belong in that club, or even that town–I was captivated. He was tall and slender, with brown eyes, a square jaw, and fluid movements. From his wrist dangled two silver bracelets, and he wore chunky silver rings on the fingers of both hands. He represented a world far from this one, of sophistication, intelligence–even glamour.

"Who is that?" I asked Jody in a loud whisper.

"A new waiter. Shane. Shane O'Neill. Goes to Queen's."

Jody knew everyone.

Within a month we were a couple, blissfully so. I had never met anyone like Shane. He was eight years my senior–26 to my 18–and was finishing his MA in Art History. His specialty was Italian Renaissance Painting and he could recite endless details about themes in Italian art, all of which I listened to with feigned fascination. I couldn't believe Shane was interested in me. He said he'd never met an eighteen-year-old who owned her own house, her own car, and managed her own affairs. The fact that I was from Iceland added an extra layer of piquancy.

Shane loved to cook, and made me dinner in his well-equipped, potted-herb-lined kitchen. He introduced me to a host of culinary delights that he and his two roommates ate as a matter of course: ratatouille, artichoke hearts, Belgian chocolate, extra virgin olive oil. He insisted on having a big pepper grinder on the table at every meal ("I can't imagine a meal without freshly ground black pepper"), went a long way out of his way to buy gourmet coffee ("Can't drink that crap from the supermarket"), and kept his coffee in the fridge ("It stays fresher that way"). While I was at first slightly intimidated by Shane, I soon found that intellectually I could hold my own with him. For instance, one night at his place while making hummus–another novelty to which he introduced me–I found myself in a discussion with him about the importance of a university education.

"If you want to get anywhere these days you have to have a Masters," he said as he poured a can of chickpeas into a blender.

"I'm opposed to the whole idea of having to show academic excellence in order to be taken seriously in life," I replied. "The things you learn in books aren't the only things that count."

"What things count?"

"Understanding on an emotional level. Having empathy. Or street smarts. To name a few," I said.

"Okay, but you still have to live in the world. You need a job, and for that you need that piece of paper."

"Not for all jobs."

"All jobs worth anything," he said.

"So why are you going into modelling? You don't need a piece of paper for that. Why bother with a Master's in Art History if you want to be a model?"

Shane and I had talked briefly about our future aspirations. Or, more to the point, *his* future aspirations. He planned to leave

Kingston as soon as he submitted his thesis, and Toronto was his destination of choice because that was where the modelling agencies were. He had the looks for it and spoke about his ambitions seemingly not from conceit but from a pragmatic standpoint that I found comforting–it suggested that he wasn't too self-absorbed.

"Well, I don't know if the modelling is going to work out, but I can always fall back on my Master's," he said.

"Somehow I can't see you as an art history professor," I said with a chuckle. "That's what art historians do, right? Teach other potential art history professors about the history of art?"

He grinned. "That's right. Smart girl."

Yeah, I knew I was smart. As long as I could rely on my mind, the gnawing emptiness that lurked within could be kept in check. And though I had espoused the importance of emotions and empathy, the fact of the matter was that I relied almost exclusively on my intellect in interpersonal relationships. I had no empathy for my friends who were stuck in what I perceived to be an emotional quagmire. I had little patience for people who were "weak" when it came to matters of the heart. My intellect was what fascinated Shane, not my capacity for showing emotion. And the raw truth was that I feigned my emotions because I had no access to my own feelings. I wanted Shane not for who he was, but for who he appeared to be–a gorgeous, urbane, self-assured and well-educated man. What I offered him in return was my own persona: the confident, capable, skinny and stylish home owner with a European background.

With my trip to Iceland scheduled for five weeks hence, Shane and I threw ourselves into our relationship with the sort of freewheeling abandon that is easy when a separation is imminent. I was excited to be going to Iceland and gushed about its beauty: the extraordinary places I had visited, the sublime summer nights that never grew dark, the wild partying people got up to, the hot springs you could bathe in naked, the energy, culture, waterfalls, glaciers, mountains, vistas.

"It sounds incredible," he said after one of my lengthy exposés. "You have to take pictures–lots of them. I want to see all that."

I knew I did–not only for Shane, but for every other person who had said they wanted to see photos from Iceland after listening to my enumerations. The only problem was that I didn't own a camera, and told him so.

"Jeez, that's a bummer. I wish I had one to lend you."

We were in his kitchen, tidying up after one of his fabulous meals.

"I've been trying to figure out who could lend me theirs for a full month in the middle of the summer, but amazingly I have thought of no one," I said with a wry grin.

"Amazingly," he echoed and we smiled at each other. I loved that he got my sardonic side. "Don't your parents have one?"

I shrugged. "My mom's husband does, but he wouldn't lend it to me. Even though he never uses it." I did not tell Shane that the main reason Richard did not use his camera was because he could not stand spending money on developing photos that were out of focus, or where someone had their eyes closed.

"Why won't he lend it to you?"

"He hates my guts."

He put his arm around me, pulling me close. "How could anyone hate your guts?" he said, nuzzling my neck.

I put my arms around his waist and laid my face against his chest. I loved the way he smelled, and how safe I felt in his presence.

❦

Three days before I was to leave for Iceland, something extraordinary occurred.

It was a Friday evening and I was strolling back to Jim and Klara's. As I was intent on leaving Kingston I had rented my house out to university students, and Klara had invited me to stay with her and Jim until I left for Iceland. The evening was warm and fragrant, the crickets chirped, and the wooden street lamps cast gentle circles of light on the cracked sidewalks. I had been out for drinks with friends and was pleasantly buzzed. Approaching the house, I glanced at the white brick building on the other side of the street where Erin and Kevin and Piper had lived–they had moved to Vancouver a few years back. My involvement in their family felt like another lifetime now. The person I was today had no relationship to the little girl who had skedaddled out of there on New Year's Eve and never looked back, save for the one trip to retrieve her treasured Donny Osmond album. I was proud of that little girl. She had done what she needed to do in order to ensure her own safety, and had not hesitated, despite the heartbreak of leaving behind that precious dog–Piper.

I was about to turn away when an object in the gutter caught my eye. It lay there among shrivelled leaves and other debris–black, vaguely resembling a shiny stone a little larger than my fist. I moved closer; squinted.

No.

Raising myself up I looked all around, half expecting someone to jump out of a bush, yelling *surprise!* But the road was deserted save for a woman getting out of a car three blocks away. Stooping down, I carefully picked up the object. It was in a black vinyl case that snapped shut at the back. Out of an opening in the side hung a loop strap. Across the bulging front was an inscription: MINOLTA.

Glancing around once more, I opened the case and removed a camera. It was a newish model with a focus lens. I stared at it, unsure of what to do. Should I leave it there? Take it inside? Someone had lost it, for sure, and would eventually come looking for it. Yet, if I left it out here, a car might drive over it, or someone else would pick it up.

I took it inside. Klara and Jim were in bed, and the house was quiet. Sitting down on the stairs in their front hall I contemplated this bizarre find. It was crazy. I had spent weeks racking my brain for someone who might be able to lend me a camera, and now one had appeared, right in front of the house where I was staying, three days before my departure. Could someone have placed it there for me to find? Theoretically, yes ... but who? And anyway, if someone had decided to surprise me by lending me a camera, leaving it out in the gutter would have been an extremely bad idea.

The following morning, I showed the camera to Klara, explaining what had happened. After some deliberation we decided that I should take it with me to Iceland. She would place a lost & found ad in the Kingston Whig Standard, and if someone claimed it she would say that I had taken the liberty of borrowing it for a month. If not ... well, then she supposed it was mine to keep.

No one claimed the camera. I took it to Iceland, and used it well. In fact I owned it for many years, and it accompanied me on numerous journeys.

That incident on that warm June evening in 1981 gave me my first inkling that a power beyond my own understanding existed, one that would quietly fulfil my most ardent needs, and lovingly bestow upon me gifts that I did not have to earn. It was almost as though, at this important juncture in my life, an omniscient entity was making its presence felt with a quiet assurance–manifested through a camera in a black vinyl case that lay in the gutter for me to find.

PART II

I thought once how Theocritus had sung
Of the sweet years, the dear and wished for years,
Who each one in a gracious hand appears
To bear a gift for mortals, old or young:
And, as I mused it in his antique tongue,
I saw, in gradual vision through my tears,
The sweet, sad years, the melancholy years,
Those of my own life, who by turns had flung
A shadow across me. Straightway I was 'ware,
So weeping, how a mystic Shape did move
Behind me, and drew me backward by the hair,
And a voice said in mastery, while I strove, ...
Guess now who holds thee?'—Death,' I said. But there,
The silver answer rang ... Not Death, but Love.'

— *Elizabeth Barrett Browning, Sonnets from the Portuguese*

CHAPTER 16

It was strange, this returning to my homeland and family at intervals of a year or more. Each time I went back, so much had happened. I had changed, or they had, or our circumstances. I noticed it in my grandparents, who were growing older–lines in their faces, or changes in their bodies that would not have been so striking had I witnessed them gradually, from day to day.

Things had changed with my father, too. He had a new family–a new partner, Vera, with whom he had a daughter, Hekla, who by now was a toddler. I had met Vera three years earlier, just after she and my father began dating, when I went back to Iceland for the summer. She was only seven years older than me, stylish and glamorous, with a dazzling smile. At fifteen I had been in awe of her, and she completely won me over when she gave me some of her hand-me-downs to take home–though they were going out of style in Iceland, they were still very trendy back in Canada, and earned me a whole lot of fashion cred.

We next met a year-and-a-half later when I went to Iceland for Christmas. The relationship between her and my father had been taken to the next level by then: they had a new baby, and had just finished restoring an old house that they had moved into. I stayed with them during that visit and everything was grand. Vera and I got along very well and were more like gossiping girlfriends than any semblance a of stepmother-daughter relationship–which seemed perfectly natural, given the close proximity of our ages.

Yet when I arrived in the summer of 1981, things were different. My father and Vera were building an addition onto their house, and were living in borrowed accommodation. My sister Jana–my father and Lísa's daughter, who by this time was eight–was spending the summer with our father. Within an hour of entering their home I could tell that my father and Vera's relationship was very strained. Over the ensuing week I experienced my father as perpetually distracted, and any time he spent with me alone seemed to aggravate Vera greatly. There were silences as taut as bowstrings, caustic offhand remarks, and an abiding hostility in the air.

I craved a sense of belonging, yet my very presence there seemed to precipitate strife and discontent. I felt awful and ashamed and had no idea what to do, so I withdrew to my room and tried to make myself invisible. I slept a lot, finding solace in slumber. Yet staying out of the way did not seem to rectify anything, and the tension only grew worse. In the end it erupted in a fierce argument between Vera and me. What caused it I can no longer recall–no doubt some trivial spark that, landing in a tinderbox of smothered feelings, caused an explosion. My father was not at home, so I rushed to my room where, trembling, I threw some belongings in a bag, then left the house and caught the bus to my grandparents'.

As ever, they opened the door wide to me. My grandmother listened to my account of what had happened, and did not judge or take sides. I asked if I could stay with them until I talked to my father. "Of course," was the answer–I was always welcome.

My grandmother made me a bed downstairs in the apartment where I had lived for the first few years of my life, when my mother and father were still together, that now served primarily as a plant nursery for my grandfather's seedlings. I did not know what I would say to my father when he came, but held on to vague hope that he would step up for me. When he did come, the next day, he looked fatigued and downcast. Sitting across from me at a table that had once belonged to my great-grandfather, he told me that it would probably be best if I did not come back to stay with him and Vera. My grandparents would let me stay with them until I left for Canada, which was in about three days' time.

I told myself it didn't matter, that I was better off there than in the powder keg that was my father and Vera's home. Yet deep down I felt shattered. I now understand that I had got through the emotional wasteland of my years in Canada by imagining that back in Iceland there were people who loved me, cared for me and supported me. This notion, that I had clung to ever since my mother first insisted I go with her to visit Klara at the age of five, was my amulet. I had told myself over and over that my father was somewhere waiting for me, and I could go back there at any time. I would then start to feel alive again. It was there that my life awaited me.

I had survived abandonment by my mother by telling myself that my father would never abandon me. That he was *there* and would always have my back.

Yet here, now, was my father, telling me I had no place with him. That he did not want me to come back. That he wanted me to stay away.

In the space of a few minutes, the delusion that had sustained me was shattered.

I had been walking a tightrope above an abyss, and I now felt it slacken.

CHAPTER 17

WHEN OUR LIVES HAVE been constructed on a lie, truth is brutal. It annihilates our illusions, and ushers in the dark night of the soul. Some illusions die quickly; others long, painful, drawn-out deaths. And when they have formed the very foundation on which our identities rest, it can feel like the end of life itself.

In my illusion, my real life had always been in Iceland. That was where the warmth resided, the joy, the opportunity for becoming. Canada was a place where I put in time–it was not my real life. Like the little girl transplanted at the age of five, subconsciously I had always been waiting to return home. And now that it was time for me to enter adulthood, to embark on my own life, I had gone to Iceland to claim it ... and found nothing.

Except the only thing that mattered: the truth.

I returned to Canada, of course, for that was the only home I knew. I moved in with Klara and Jim temporarily, and reconnected with Shane. To any outside observer I probably looked like I knew what I was doing, but in truth I was utterly lost, the void inside me big enough to drive a tank through. All I knew was that I could not stay in Kingston–I had to get away. Like legions of lost souls the world over, I looked to the nearest metropolis to embrace me into its fold. Toronto was less than three hours away by car, and seemed to hold the promise of salvation. It was where Shane was headed, and it was as good a place as any to try to find my life.

My mother had changed much since becoming a full-time farmer. She paid limited attention to her appearance now–gone were the high heels, the skirts, the makeup. Her clothes were unflattering, and not always clean. She had taken to cutting her own hair, and it was cropped close to her scalp. She had put on some weight, and had adopted a kind of permanent defiance, like her lack of concern with her appearance was a subtle "fuck-you"–to the patriarchy, to the world, to someone.

"What are you planning to do out there?" she asked indifferently as she filled the kettle with water. I had been back in Canada for just over a week and had driven out to see her. I had a sense that she was preoccupied, and not really that concerned with my answer–as though by leaving Kingston I was stepping out of her sphere of interest.

"I don't know yet," I said, "take a year off, figure out what I want to do." My voice sounded small, and I did not like it. Something was changing in me. Since I had been back I had noticed a strange buzzing in my brain, like a white kind of noise that robbed me of rest. I was tired all the time, yet had trouble sleeping. I woke in the early morning with an electric charge running through my body that made it impossible to get back to sleep. My mind was in overdrive all the time, and I would lie awake with thoughts rushing through it at breakneck speed. I had no words to describe what I felt, had I been inclined to share my feelings with anyone–which I was not, as they deviated so sharply from the persona I was used to presenting to the world, and to myself.

And now, here at the farm, it felt like a strange dynamic had formed between my mother and me, like we were made of nothing but edges. Inside of me I felt a nagging guilt, as though I had gravely disappointed her.

"Well, we all need to find ourselves," she replied, not looking at me. I bristled. I did not know if she had always made these sweeping statements that suggested she had omniscient knowledge, or if I had just started noticing. They had about them a grandeur that I found both haughty and abrasive. In the past I had taken strange comfort in accepting everything my mother said or did without question. Now it seemed to me that these imperious proclamations rendered everyone's unique experiences trite and banal, including mine. As though my mother was some ultimate authority, and everyone else a fool.

She invited me to stay for dinner, but I declined, since I preferred to leave before Richard came home. Besides, I had plans with Shane, though I did not tell her that. I felt a resistance in me, as though I had to erect a barrier to protect my relationship with Shane, to keep it as removed from her as I possibly could.

I had a lead on a shared apartment in Toronto through an acquaintance in Kingston, so in early September I threw some belongings into the back of my car and set off to seek my fortune.

Shane had not yet submitted his thesis and had to stay in Kingston for a few more weeks. We agreed that, assuming the flat worked out, he would come and stay with me when he had completed his studies, while he was getting himself oriented. Neither of us had broached the subject of moving in together–it seemed a bit too early in our relationship for that discussion.

The shared flat was in a semi-detached house in the Cabbagetown neighbourhood of Toronto, so named because poor immigrants who settled there in the 1840s had grown cabbages in their front yards. It was on the second and third floors of an old brownstone, and had four bedrooms–two large on the top floor, two smaller on the lower–plus a living area, and a bright kitchen with a gorgeous window alcove set into the leafy branches of a maple tree. A woman a couple of years older than me–Geraldine, Gerry for short–occupied one of the two spacious bedrooms on the upper floor of the apartment, while the other large room belonged to a guy named John whom I only met once in the space of five months. I settled into one of two smaller rooms on the lower floor, which came furnished with a bed, a dresser and a small bedside table.

Cabbagetown had only a few years earlier been a slum, but many of the Victorian townhouses had been restored to their former grandeur and sold to wealthy new owners. This fancy part of the neighbourhood was limited to around ten square blocks–a small haven of prosperity in a downtown area that was still largely populated by the disenfranchised. Inside this oasis of affluence, a village-like atmosphere had been manufactured, with specially-designed street signs, one very trendy corner shop selling "Quality Foodstuffs" at about triple the price of everywhere else, and the Riverdale Farm–a real working farm surrounded by a green park, where the upscale denizens of the area could introduce their children to domesticated animals and purchase free-range eggs for their weekend brunches. Beyond the borders of this Shangri-la the misfits still roamed: prostitutes, pimps, addicts and the homeless.

Our house sat on a strip that divided the gentrified section of Cabbagetown from the housing projects to the south known as Regent Park, known for its violence and high rates of domestic abuse. We rented from a nonprofit housing co-op that owned a few properties along our block and the next. The co-op had moved in just before the transformation of the area began, and now provided regular folks like Gerry and me with affordable rent in an affluent neighbourhood.

I had expected the strange mental stress I had been experiencing to go away in a week or two, but that did not happen. I also expected that I would manage the move to Toronto with perfect ease, but in that respect, too, I was wrong. Much to my dismay I felt overwhelmed by everything. When I sat down to try to figure out what to do now that I was there, I found that I could barely form a coherent thought. My mind was all in a muddle. I would have to get a job, and waitressing in a restaurant seemed to be the best option. Yet even the ambition to look for that kind of work eluded me. I got up in the morning determined to go out and search for something, then spent half the day sitting in the kitchen drinking tea and staring at the classifieds. I had never felt such uncertainty about the decisions I needed to make–from the smallest, like what clothes I wanted to put on that day, to the largest, like where I should apply for a job. This person who slouched around the apartment feeling ashamed of her own lack of clarity and initiative was a complete stranger to me. She was worlds removed from the competent young woman who had so deftly managed all her affairs back in Kingston.

I didn't understand what was happening to me.

One day, wandering aimlessly up Yonge Street, I saw a sign in a restaurant window: WAITRESS WANTED. Taking a deep breath, I pushed through the door and said I wanted to apply. The manager glanced quickly at my application, spoke to me while looking more at my chest than my face, and gave me the job without asking to see references. The restaurant was called Piranha and it was a hip little spot that served food during the day and morphed into a bar at night. I was put on lunches. I lied and said I'd waitressed before, but quickly grew to regret it since I found it impossible to manage everything when it got busy. My first shift was a nightmare–by the time I got home I was dead on my feet and had no memory of half of it. My second shift was not much better; my mind actually blanked out, I kept forgetting things, and a customer complained to Jack, the manager, that I was trying to lay claim to my own tip when I gave him the wrong change back.

I had only been there for two weeks when Jack sat me down and fired me. It wasn't working out, he said. They needed someone with more skill. In my old life I would have shrugged it off; now it felt like an indictment of my worth–not just as a waitress, but as a person. I felt like an utter failure.

Shane called me the following day to say that he was coming up that weekend and was looking forward to seeing my new place. He asked if I'd be working, and I told him I quit–I couldn't bear for him to know that I had been fired, that I couldn't even waitress properly. The day he was set to arrive I was a nervous wreck, and to steady my nerves kept frantically busy–cleaning the apartment, vacuuming and dusting, stashing away things that were lying about, hoping Gerry wouldn't get offended. When I was done I stood in the middle of the living room and tried to imagine how Shane would see it; if he would approve. My gaze fell on a poster of a kitten hanging on a rope with the caption "Hang in there, baby". I thought of my baby Dexter, who had not been seen for several weeks. I had taken him out to the farm when I cleared out my apartment in Kingston, intending to leave him there until I figured out my next move. When I went to the farm last time I had been eager to see Dexter, scoop him up, bury my face in his fur, listen to his purring. But no Dexter had greeted me, and my mother informed me that he had disappeared shortly after I left for Iceland. "The bears probably got him out in the woods," she said, evidently unaware that I might find this distressing. I had been upset, yet still held out hope that Dexter might return. Poor Dexter, who'd had to do what I refused to do–live with my mother and Richard on the farm. Maybe he had tried to find his way back to me, and wound up coming to the house only to find new people living there.

The doorbell buzzed, jolting me from my reverie. I bolted down the stairs to the front door. Shane was standing on the stoop, designer bag in hand, wearing jeans and a tailored blazer. He dropped the bag and put his arms around me.

"Hey," he whispered into my ear.

"Hey," I whispered back.

In the living room he turned a full circle. "So this is it, huh? Not bad. I see I'll have to bring my stereo, though." He grinned.

I exhaled, and smiled at him. He had said he liked it–sort of. "Yes. You will," I said.

He put his arms around me again, lifting me from the ground like I was a little girl. "I'm glad that's settled," he said quietly. "Now how about showing me to our room?"

Three weeks later, Shane had submitted his thesis, come to Toronto, and Moved In. The day after he arrived I went out in the morning and returned to find his stereo sitting on the makeshift red brick bookcase in the living room, his clothes hung in my closet, and my things rearranged in the dresser so that he could have two drawers to himself. He had taken down a poster for The Nutcracker Suite that had hung on the wall and replaced it with a Peruvian wall hanging. His South American bedspread was draped across the bed. An Albert Camus novel that I recalled from his bedside in Kingston lay face down and open on the milk crate that acted as a bedside table. Clearly it was taking him an awful long time to finish.

A few days later I came home from picking up some groceries and found him sitting at the kitchen table reading The Globe and Mail and sipping coffee.

"Hi," he said, glancing up.

"Hi."

"Do you want the rest of this coffee?" He gestured to his push-down coffee brewer.

"Um, no thanks."

He stood up as I started putting things away, leaning backwards against the kitchen counter and crossing his arms. "I just got a call from the Shoot! agency," he said. "I took over my portfolio last week. They're going to sign me."

"Oh," I said, straightening up. "Wow. Congratulations. That's good."

"I applied for some wait jobs, too," he continued. "They were really positive down at the Rivoli on Queen West. Do you know it?"

"I've seen it."

"It seems like a cool place. They have live music all nights. They're going to call me tomorrow."

"Great."

I waited for Shane to ask me how my day had been and what I had been up to, but instead he just stood there watching me unpack the grocery bags. I couldn't help noticing that he did not offer to help me put stuff away. I wondered what it would be like to have even an ounce of his confidence–he seemed so unshakable; his sense of entitlement so absolute.

He went into the living room and flopped down on the couch, picking up a magazine that was lying there. "Oh, by the way, I invited some people over for dinner on Saturday," he called, as though just remembering.

I had a surge of anxiety. "Who?"

"An old friend from school. Pete. I ran into him today on the subway. He's a banker. Him and his wife."

I turned back to the groceries, wishing I could be rid of this perpetual dread. Back in Kingston I had been the exotic Icelandic girl who owned her own house and car and was intellectually savvy, unfazed by most things. Now I had been stripped of that role and felt raw and exposed. Worse, I had no sense of what was normal and legitimate in our relationship. Like, should he not have consulted with me before inviting his friends over to our place for dinner? Or perhaps checked whether Gerry had something planned?

Was I making a big deal out of nothing?

"Okay, great," I said, with less enthusiasm than I'd hoped to convey.

He did not seem to notice.

The stretches of time when I felt like the person I used to be, who was witty and smart and self-assured, grew shorter and shorter, and were replaced by someone who lived in constant need for Shane's approval, and fear of not living up to his standards. Of not being as good, as perfect, as Shane. Of not being good enough *for* Shane. I wanted to make him proud. Wanted to make him happy. But I couldn't help feeling, constantly, that I wasn't enough. I who had always been so clear-headed and so able to hold my own in any conversation now felt like my intellect had been sunk in a swamp. It took colossal effort to deal with even the most banal situations, like how to respond to quips or offhand remarks. I felt stilted and awkward, my brain sluggish and dull. My sense of humour was gone. I felt no joy.

Shane had started working at the Rivoli and really liked it, especially the people he was working with. He liked them so much that often he didn't come home from work until the wee hours of the morning–five or six. By then I'd have been home from work for hours. I had a job as a hostess in a place near the Art Gallery of Ontario called Ginsberg & Wong, that served a bizarre fusion of Jewish and Chinese cuisine and was primarily known for its humongous food portions, half of which went directly into the trash during any given shift.

As my anxiety grew and my self-esteem plummeted, my physical health began to suffer. I had stopped menstruating, yet my stomach was constantly bloated. I had cramps in my belly, pain in my lower back, and felt nauseous much of the time. The brain fog was getting worse, and my sense of inferiority around Shane was sometimes so great that I wanted nothing more than to crawl into bed and not speak to anyone. I was terrified that he would see through to who I really was on the inside, yet keeping up the façade of a strong, competent person was becoming more and more difficult all the time. I was sure he was getting bored with me, since I never had anything interesting to say. Also, I started to have a nagging suspicion that he was cheating on me–he talked a lot about a girl he worked with named Sharon, with whom he seemed besotted. Were they just friends, or something more? Was I paranoid to associate his late nights with his admiration for Sharon, or perfectly sane? I didn't know–my sense of reality was all screwed up. I didn't know what was real any more.

One day I woke up with an excruciating pain in my lower belly, that would not go away. I had the name of a family doctor that had been recommended by my GP back in Kingston, and called her office to see about an appointment. The receptionist informed me that she'd just had a cancellation, and could I come at 1 p.m. that afternoon?

I showed up at the appointed time, and was ushered into the office of Dr. Lennox, a big-boned woman with light-brown hair, who I guessed to be in her early thirties. After a brief chat about my symptoms–which over the previous two hours had lessened somewhat–she set about examining me. When she had finished she invited me to sit across the desk from her, and told me that she had not been able to find anything definitively wrong with me, but that I might have an infection in my fallopian tubes.

"When was your last period?" she asked.

I told her I had not menstruated for several months.

She looked at me, not unkindly. "You're very thin. That may be a reason."

I dropped my eyes, as though by doing so I might prevent her from seeing the mess I was on the inside.

"But what about this pain I've been having?"

"I'm going to prescribe antibiotics, in case you have an infection." She paused. "Is it possible that your symptoms are psychosomatic?"

I opened my mouth to blurt out my denial, but closed it again. Why was I so afraid of her seeing me?

"Do you have any symptoms of depression? Any … trouble sleeping, low self-esteem, lack of motivation, difficulty with making decisions …?"

I stared at her. In four pithy phrases she had more or less summed up my entire state of being. But … depression? Was that what depression felt like? I had never thought of myself as a person who got depressed. I didn't feel particularly sad or morose, which is what I thought depression was. I just felt … not like myself.

I nodded.

"Can you tell me when this started?"

"Um …" It had started when I got back to Canada from Iceland. Just as I was moving to Toronto. "About two months ago, I guess."

Concern was etched on her face. "And these symptoms I described …?"

I nodded. "All those things," I said.

"I see. Anything else?"

"This feeling of mental stress, like my thoughts are all over the place and I can't stop them. I feel confused and really slow to grasp things. And I'm so insecure and afraid all the time. I feel like I want to disappear."

She frowned. "Are you having suicidal thoughts?"

I shrugged. "Not exactly. More like … I don't want anyone to see me. It's hard to explain."

She nodded.

"Things haven't been going all that well in my relationship. I think that may be the problem," I added.

"Sometimes our relationships are not the root of our discomfort," she said. "The root may be something deeper, and it is important to get to the root if we want to avoid relationships that hurt us."

I nodded slowly. It made sense.

She hesitated. "Would you ... like to speak to someone about these things? A professional?"

I swallowed. "Do you think I should?"

She nodded emphatically. "Yes," she said. "I think you should."

CHAPTER 18

IT WAS A COLD DAY in mid-December when I headed to my first psychiatric appointment at St. Michael's hospital in downtown Toronto. It had taken more than a month for me to get the appointment, and during that time, at my mother's behest, I had ended my relationship with Shane. I had driven down to her farm where she had outlined the problem for me: Shane was clearly an egomaniac, and I needed to get out of that relationship, stat. Fortified by her indignation, had returned to Toronto to tell him I did not think things between us were working out. I remember shaking inside as I told him, not knowing if I was seeing things clearly, or if I was just doing what my mother expected of me.

To my surprise he was in perfect agreement, and offered to move out right away.

So, on this gloomy morning, with flurries blowing across the sidewalk in front of me, my step was light. I felt infinitely better since Shane had moved out. Gone was my crippling insecurity; no longer did I feel so small.

The psychiatrist to whom Dr. Lennox had referred me worked out of the outpatient clinic at the hospital. A receptionist invited me to take a seat in the waiting area, which consisted of a few chairs in front of double doors that marked the entrance to the hospital ward. A few minutes later a man appeared through the doors and called my name. He was small and had a protruding belly, dark skin and nimble movements. I followed him to an office just down the hall, where he introduced himself as Dr. Diamond. He gestured to a bolstered chair across from him, and offered me coffee. I declined, but accepted a glass of water.

"So," he said kindly, settling into a chair opposite me, "what brings you to see me today?"

"Well," I began, clasping my hands together, "I made the appointment about a month ago when I was in a relationship that was having a bad effect on me, but I've since ended it and I'm feeling a lot better. In fact," I chuckled conspiratorially, "I don't even think I need to be here."

"I see," he said amiably "Yet you kept the appointment. Why?"

I had not expected that.

"I guess maybe I needed confirmation that I really am better," I said, a tad flustered. "I ... think the problem is that I'm not cut out for relationships. I always feel better on my own."

He nodded. "Well, maybe you can start by telling me why you made the appointment four weeks ago."

And so, I told him about Shane and how he had made me feel afraid and inferior, of his confidence that took away all *my* confidence, that I suspected him of screwing around, and how I kept getting more and more confused, with all these bouts of mental stress. "But, as I said," I concluded, "I'm a lot better now that we've broken up. I feel like I've dealt with the problem."

I waited for him to applaud me, to tell me I'd done good, that I'd handled the situation exactly right. But instead he cocked his head and said: "Tell me about yourself."

I was perplexed. "I just did."

"Well, I know you were in a relationship with … ?"

"Shane."

"Shane. But I don't know much about you. About your background, where you grew up, your family … that sort of thing."

I felt mildly annoyed. What was the point of that? I had made the appointment to get confirmation that breaking it off with Shane had been the right thing to do because he was a jerk. What did *my* life have to do with anything?

I glanced at my watch. Half an hour left. Fine–I might as well stay to the end of the session.

I began with the highlights: parents divorced, moved to Canada with my mother, started living on my own when I was sixteen, owned a house and car, was now taking some time off to figure out what I wanted to do with my life. He listened, nodding and asking the occasional question. Then, with some probing, he managed to further glean that I didn't get along with my stepfather, I'd had a fight with my father's girlfriend, for the last couple of years I'd been obsessed with my weight, and that I'd been having problems with my health.

He settled back in his chair and glanced at the notes he had made. The hour was almost up. I kept my eyes fixed on him, waiting for the verdict. I fully expected that he would marvel at my competence and maturity, present me with a clean bill of health, and send me on my way.

"Have you ever heard the term 'mental floss'?" he said, looking up over his glasses.

What the…?

"No," I answered.

"It's a pun on dental floss, which we use to maintain our dental health. But we also need to maintain our mental health, and psychotherapy is one way to do that. It helps you gain a better awareness of yourself, which in turn helps you in other areas of your life."

"Ah ok," I said, wondering what this had to do with me.

He paused. "I think you could benefit from psychotherapy, even though your relationship is finished."

"Oh!" I was taken aback. Was he suggesting that I was crazy?

"Therapy isn't just for crazy people," he said, as though reading my thoughts. "It's also for people who want to make better choices. It might help you avoid hurtful relationships in the future."

I considered this. I didn't care about my future relationships: as far as I was concerned I was not going to have any. I was done. Yet knowing what I did *not* want was not the same as knowing what I *did* want.

"Will it help me decide what I want to do with my life?" I asked.

"I can't promise anything, but I believe so, yes," he said.

"And it is covered by my health insurance?"

"Yes, it is."

I thought for a moment, then said, "Okay."

I began meeting with Dr. Diamond every Saturday morning at his home in a north Toronto suburb, where he saw a handful of clients. His consulting room was warm and welcoming, painted in peach tones, with a wall-to-wall carpet, a desk made of dark wood, and African masks on the wall. Occasionally I would come upon his two young children playing in the front yard, who would look at me shyly and keep out of the way, likely on their parents' instructions.

In the beginning it just felt like talking, yet it soon became evident that our meetings were about much more than that. They were surgery. I came to see that my decision to get involved with Shane had not been a random toss of the die, but had been governed by a blueprint of conditioning that began forming the day I was conceived. I needed to sink deep into the murky waters of my subconscious and let the pent-up feelings buried there pass through me so that I could begin to take charge of my life.

Thus began the unspooling of my self. Time, as it turned out, did not heal all wounds–it merely covered them over. Now the scabs were being torn off, laying bare all the feelings I had put on ice and refused to admit–terror, paranoia, insecurity, self-condemnation … all rushed out at me now, clamouring for attention.

Like a wounded animal, my instinct was to isolate. I crawled into the safest space I could find–my bedroom, which was now on the top floor of the house as John, the all-but-invisible tenant, had moved out. Interactions that had previously been simple–lunch or coffee with people I knew, basic conversations with shopkeepers about the weather–were now an ordeal. I had no sense of who I was, no sense of myself in the world; I had no emotional connection to a past, and no vision of the future. It was like spiritual amnesia. I looked at things but did not see; listened, but did not hear. Something as simple as reading a book was impossible–the words were made up of symbols on a page that I could not connect to anything. It was like someone had come into my life and turned off all the lights, plunging me into darkness.

The most terrible part was the sense of having been flayed, as though I was walking around with no skin, raw and exposed and excruciatingly vulnerable. Every single person on the street terrified me. In my mind's eye they were huge and strong and powerful, while I was small and utterly defenceless. I cowered under their gazes, which I was sure condemned and judged me in the harshest possible way. My old nemesis from the house in Bayridge, the one that had watched my every move through the small window in the front door, now existed in every person I encountered–on the street, in a shop, in a restaurant. Every glance, every look, even by people I did not know, brought on a torrent of self-hatred.

I was acutely conscious that I must not show how weak I felt. I was sure that, were anyone to see my injuries, I would be in mortal danger. So I kept up appearances as best I could. The fact was, of course, that I had been keeping up appearances for years–the only difference now was that I was aware of the truth beneath the facade, whereas in the past I had been oblivious. And so, I continued to play the role that I had honed so well. I went to work, shopped for food, rode the streetcar, and appeared "normal"–yet beneath it all, I was falling apart.

"We call it projection," said Dr. Diamond. "Have you heard that term before?"

It was a Saturday morning and I sat pressed into the corner of a large upholstered armchair in his consulting room, wearing a baggy sweatshirt with a hood, and loose jeans. I had been telling him about my fear of random strangers on the street, my dread of their judgement and scorn.

I shook my head.

"It means that just because you feel something, it isn't necessarily real. In fact, very often it is not. Imagine that you are a film projector. The film is inside of you, but as you move through life you project your film onto other people. What you are seeing is not objective reality, but the film playing inside your own self."

"Okay," I said.

"Often when we carry strong feelings inside of us we are like a film projector, and the screen is other people. We believe the action is with them–that they are thinking certain things or acting in certain ways–but what is really happening is that we are projecting our own feelings onto them."

"So … when I think they are hating on me, I am really hating on myself?"

He smiled, and for a moment I thought he looked proud of me. "Yes, that is exactly what I mean."

I nodded, allowing this to sink in.

"Sometimes when we feel guilt, or shame, or self-condemnation, we believe others are judging us, when we are really judging ourselves." He paused, then asked, "How do you feel when you are here, with me? Do you feel that I am judging you harshly?"

"Yes," I said, without hesitation. "I mean ... intellectually I know you probably aren't because you're my therapist ... but my feeling is that you are."

"And when you think I am judging you, how does that make you feel?"

"Bad. Like I need to be perfect."

"And what would happen if you were not perfect?"

"You would reject me."

"Would that be so terrible?"

I reflected. "I don't know."

He sat quiet for a moment, as though waiting for me to say something more. When I did not, he continued. "No one likes rejection. But we have two choices. We can think, 'He has his own reasons for not wanting to have me around, and it does not diminish my worth as a person. It just means that this isn't a good fit.' That would be the healthy response. Or you could project something onto me, like, say, your father's rejection of you, and believe you have to be perfect for me to love and accept you. That is your own projection and it doesn't have anything to do with reality. The reality is that, today, you–Alda–are an adult, and capable of finding people who want to be with you, who have things in common with you, and who don't reject you." He paused. "Do you see?"

I nodded. I was learning so much. Each session with Dr. Diamond was like a lesson in humanity's response to pain. In learning about myself, I was learning about everyone else, too–how we shut down parts of ourselves when we are traumatised, how that can be a necessary survival response at the time, but how it does not serve us well when the danger has passed. I was learning that, unless I picked up the broken parts of myself and put them back together, I would never be happy. I could live in the biggest house in Toronto, wear the trendiest clothes, drive the most expensive car, have the most desirable husband … but unless I became whole, none of it would matter. I had to seek peace, joy, contentment within myself. That was my task now. To recover the person I was destined to be before my life went off the rails.

The deeper I moved into therapy, the worse I started to feel. Today, decades later, I know that this is normal–that when you rip the scabs off old wounds, painful emotions that had been buried underneath rush out at you like bats from a deep, dark cellar. Because the process necessarily involves regression into the psyche of the child, the feelings usually feel overwhelming and terrifying, as they did to the little girl who struggled to suppress these forces that threatened to tear her apart. Yet I did not understand any of this at the time. I simply felt trapped in a whirlpool of emotions, struggling to stay afloat, trying not to drown.

Most days were bad, but some were worse than others. One morning I woke, sick with inner malaise. The humming inside my brain was intense, my body seethed with a corrosive energy, and the prospect of leaving my room to go outside brought an onset of terrible panic. I crouched on the floor and put my forehead down, rocking back and forth like a baby. I needed comfort, I needed consoling. I needed my mother.

On the landing between my room and Gerry's there was a phone. I crawled to the door and quietly opened it, just enough to pull the phone inside. Then I dialled my mother's number.

"Mamma," I said in an unsteady voice when she picked up the phone.

"Hi," she said, with a hint of surprise. "Are you all right?"

"No," I whimpered, then tried to explain. I told her I was in so much pain–a pain that I had never experienced before, a mental pain that felt as horrible as any flesh wound. I told her I was terrified to go outside. I told her I didn't want to die, but I also didn't want to live. I told her I didn't know what to do, and that I needed help.

She listened, and even though I could not see her I had the feeling that my words were hitting that glass surrounding her, behind which she resided. When I finished I waited, trembling, for a response. I did not know how she would take it. I had never talked to my mother this way, had never made myself so vulnerable, and it occurred to me that I was afraid of her reaction–afraid that she would not approve of me like this. I was weak now, and my mother had shown me that she abhorred weakness. My father had been weak, she said, and she had made no secret of how much she despised that in him.

"Oh, it's normal," she said cheerfully. "I went through this at your age. You should have seen me in my twenties; I was so insecure. It's something everyone goes through."

She made it sound so insignificant–and no doubt she was right. I wanted to believe that. After all, she had gone through the same thing. She was the authority, and if she said my feelings were not that bad, then surely they were not that bad.

And yet ... what *was* all this inside of me? Were these feelings not real? Was I dramatizing something that was, in fact, nothing?

"*How* did you get through it?" I asked, knowing I sounded desperate.

"I had you," she said breezily. "I couldn't spend time wallowing; I had a child to take care of."

Wallowing. Was that what I was doing?

There was a pause, in which I heard my mother take a drink of something. "What does the doctor say?" she asked.

I put my back against the side of the bed and pulled my knees up to my chest. "He says it's a byproduct of opening up old wounds," I said. "In part because I come from a broken home and did not grow up with my father."

She made a sound somewhere between a snort and a chuckle. "Well, I grew up without a father, and I'm all right," she said disparagingly. "You must be very sensitive."

There it was: my mother's diagnosis. I was sensitive. That was the problem.

I felt a crushing sense of erasure.

"I have some news," she said, the tone of her voice completely changed. "I was going to wait until the next time you came down to tell you, but since I have you on the phone ..."

"Oh?" I said feebly. "What?"

"I'm pregnant."

If she had told me that the apple tree in her yard had started to grow pineapples I could not have been more surprised. The thought had literally never crossed my mind that my mother and Richard might have a child together. I do not know why–after all, they were married and had no child of their own, even though between them they had five. I suppose I had always assumed that five was enough for them. Or perhaps it was that I had never heard my mother mention, even in passing, that she wanted another child.

"Are you there?" she asked.

I found my voice. "Wow," I said. "Congratulations. I didn't know you were trying for a baby."

Then she made an utterly baffling remark, the import of which I would understand only later. "Yes, since there was little chance you would have one for me, I figured I would have to do it myself."

I sat with my back against my bed, the carpet scratchy under the soles of my bare feet, feeling a seething sense that I had failed my mother by not having a child for her, and forcing her to have one all by herself.

CHAPTER 19

IT WAS A SOPORIFIC DAY in August, the sort of hot and muggy day when everything feels laboured. I was riding the streetcar home from a lunch shift at Ginsberg & Wong–I had been promoted from hostess to waitress, which I appreciated from the financial angle, on account of the tips. Yet as I had learned at Piranha all those months before, I did not do well with insanely busy lunch shifts that demanded a great deal of sharpness. I now aspired to be a bartender, which required far less running around, and offered higher wages.

Getting off the streetcar at the corner of Parliament and Gerrard I accidentally bumped into a woman who spun around and, to my surprise, exclaimed "Alda?"

"Sheila!"

Sheila had been a student at Queens University in Kingston and had worked part-time as a cocktail waitress in the same club as Shane. We had partied together a few times after hours, and I always liked her. She had a big personality, gregarious and self-assured, and she now threw her arms around me as the streetcar pulled away. "What are you doing here?" she said excitedly, "I didn't know you were in TO!"

"Yeah, yeah, I've been here about a year," I said with a grin. "I live just around the corner."

"That's crazy! I'm working as a bartender at The Freehouse."

I knew The Freehouse–it was an English pub located on Parliament Street, down in a basement, just a few houses from where I lived. I had passed it hundreds of times but had never gone in. "My shift is about to start; are you busy?" Sheila went on. "Come in with me, I'll buy you a beer. It's so nice to see you!"

I let myself be led inside, where Sheila instructed me to take a seat at the bar while she took her stuff to the back office. I cast around. Three guys were playing darts in an alcove near the front. In a separate room I could see a waiter setting up tables for dinner–that section looked more formal than the bar, with tablecloths and upholstered seats.

Sheila appeared with a cash float and, after exchanging a few words with the bartender on duty, slid it into the cash register and asked me what I would like to drink. She then filled me in on her life since we had last seen each other: she had returned to Toronto after graduation and had been bartending and picking up odd jobs in the film industry. Nearly a year ago she had started at The Freehouse but had recently found a full-time job with a production company and would be leaving in a couple of weeks. I sat quietly and listened, soothed at not having to share anything about myself, safe inside my shell.

Alas, Sheila's monologue soon ended. "So what about you–what are you up to?" she asked cheerfully, wiping glasses from the glass washer and hanging them in an overhead rack. I felt a pang of embarrassment. What, indeed, was I doing? I had planned to take a year off to figure out what I wanted to study, but now that year had passed and the subsequent school year was about to start. Sheila, I knew, was one of those judicious people who had their life all mapped out by the end of high school, then went to university and finished whatever they had decided to study without any indecision. What could I tell her? Back in Kingston, when she knew me, I'd been a different person–a "most likely to succeed" type of person. Yet here I was, waitressing in some novelty restaurant that threw away truckloads of food every day, and my greatest ambition was to move up to shaking cocktails.

"Um ... I decided to take a year to figure out what I wanted to do and, well, it's turning into two years now," I said, striving to keep my voice light. A look crossed her face, one I knew well–a mixture of pity and smugness, glossed over with feigned interest. It was a look that I had sometimes given to people in my previous incarnation, back when I thought I was infallible.

"... In the meantime, I'm waitressing," I finished.

"Oh. Where?"

I told her, adding that I didn't like it there much and that I was going to start looking for something new, ideally tending bar.

She stopped mid-wipe. "Well, that's perfect! You can have this job. It's serendipity!"

I blinked, startled by her temerity, then muttered something about probably needing to apply first. I had barely uttered the words when a lanky man of Asian descent with big glasses emerged from the door marked "Office".

"Don't worry," she said, lowering her voice, "it won't be a problem". She turned. "Jon?" The man swerved towards us. "This is my friend Alda from Kingston. She's working at Ginsberg & Wong but is looking for a new job. You should give her mine. She's a good bartender, I'll vouch for her." She glanced at me and winked.

Ten minutes later I was hired.

I settled into a full-time bartending job at The Freehouse, a restaurant-pub that had opened just over a year earlier and was owned by prominent Toronto real estate developer Joseph Brady, who had been peripherally involved in the gentrification of Cabbagetown. He was originally from England and had come up with the idea of opening a pub that was a throwback to his childhood back in Blighty–a replica of an English tavern that would cater to the upscale denizens that were moving into the area. The restaurant served upscale fare, and a jazz quartet played evenings from Thursday to Saturday. It was a cool, sophisticated venue.

At The Freehouse I had a sense of having found my tribe. Everyone who worked there had suffered a wound to the soul–they didn't actually tell me, but I could sense it, the way one broken person recognises another. There was Leila, a young woman from Estonia, whose childlike naiveté seemed to mask a deeper darkness; Jordan, a gay man from a small town in Nova Scotia, who had come to Toronto to escape stigma and who had found his people there; Harry, the head chef, brilliant and larger-than-life, who had bipolar disorder; Darlene, tall and big-boned with a clear countenance and a sweet voice, who was recovering from an eating disorder; CJ, a short man studying philosophy at the University of Toronto who had a penchant for gossip–the only one I did not trust, for he had a mean streak that occasionally bled through his perpetually upbeat demeanour; Jon, the enigmatic manager, a son of Chinese immigrants whom no one really knew very much about; and Sam, the owner's son.

Now, in early February, The Freehouse was closing for the night. Four of us were sitting at a table at the back of the dining room: Leila, Jordan, Sam and me. The evening had been busy, I was tired, my mind was in a muddle, and I was looking forward to cocooning inside my new apartment–a studio flat in a high-rise complex near the Yonge and Davisville subway station, to which I had moved about a month earlier. I had decided that I needed my own place, into which I could retreat and feel safe.

Yet I could not go home until I finished tallying up my cash and receipts–a process known as cashing out. I had to count the money in my cash tray down to the very last nickel, and I kept getting distracted by the conversation Sam and Jordan were having next to me about, of all things, *God.*

"How can you believe in a God that lets children in Ethiopia starve?" Jordan was saying.

"That is a pointless argument," Sam replied heatedly, "there are so many social and economic reasons for why the third world is the way it is. It's man who's done that, not God."

"Well, if God is so omnipotent, why doesn't he fix it?"

"You guys," Leila drawled, rolling her eyes, "it's fucking one o'clock in the morning. Can't you talk about something else?"

I got up and moved to the next table, hoping that putting some distance between us might help. I needed to concentrate.

"You're confusing God with man." Sam was intent on making his point. "You can't ascribe the traits of a human onto a divine being. It's easy to say that He should just fix it, but maybe there's a bigger plan, you know? Who are we to say what is the purpose of things?"

"So you're saying there's a purpose to the famines in Africa?"

"How the hell should I know, I'm just a human being with my limited vision and understanding."

I glanced at them. Sam and Jordan sat perfectly still, grinning at each other, clearly enjoying this mental sparring.

"Yeah, well, I don't believe in any of that crap," Jordan said dismissively. "Like all those crazy stories in the Bible … I mean, come on. Walking on water? Raising the dead?"

"Not everything in the Bible should be taken literally," Sam said. "Most things are allegorical."

"You know they found the Garden of Eden, don't you?" Leila put in.

"Yeah?" Jordan said, "Where–Rosedale?"

We all laughed.

And that is when it happened.

I looked at Sam, and suddenly felt a blow to my chest. It reminded me of the time I had put my hand on an electric fence and it was like I had been dealt a massive punch, but from the inside. Shocked, I glanced at each of the others in turn. Had something happened? Had a meteor hit Earth? Was I the only one feeling this? They were all acting perfectly normal: Leila fishing something out of her drink, Jordan leaning back with a grin, Sam saying something profound.

Then I saw it. A light around Sam, coming from within, like he was radiating from the inside. I had never seen anything like it. He was perfectly luminous. Everything in the room faded except that light, and I stared at it, enthralled. It seemed to last a very long time, though maybe it was only a few seconds–I could not judge the passage of time. Jolted back to my senses, I realised I was staring. I needed to stop. I needed to act like I didn't see. I blinked. Then I felt the trembling begin–from shock, or fear, or something else. I pushed back from the table and said "excuse me" to no one in particular, then walked slowly the few steps to the bathroom. My legs felt strangely detached from my body. I pushed through the bathroom door, then leaned my back against the wall and forced myself to breathe.

What the hell was that?

I had to get a grip. To calm down, walk myself back out there, feign normalcy. I washed my hands, just to do something, then glanced at myself in the mirror. I appeared composed–good. I went back out and sat down; no one seemed to have given any thought to my absence.

At last, I was finished with my counting. I rose carefully, like I might shatter something if I moved too abruptly. I went into the office and got my coat, taking my time putting it on–slowly buttoning the buttons, tying the belt.

"Are you leaving?" Leila asked when I returned, evidently surprised. Normally we would have sat and had another drink before I headed home.

"Yeah, I have to go."

"Can I catch a ride with you?"

"Sure." I hesitated, then took a deep breath. "Anyone else?"

"Sure, I'll take a lift if it's not out of your way," Sam said without looking up.

I perched on a chair and fidgeted with a paper napkin–tearing it into narrow strips, then braiding them while the others gathered up their stuff. When we were ready to go we filed up the narrow staircase at the back of the bar that led to a small parking lot out back and an alley beyond. A layer of fresh snow covered everything like a weighted blanket, muffling sound and making our light prattle sound curiously intimate. A battered wooden streetlight cast a warm circle of light on the ground. The sky was orange.

Sam needed to be dropped off first, so he held the passenger door open for Leila to climb in the back, then got in the front. Jordan waved goodbye–he always rode his bicycle to work, in summer and winter. I got out the snow brush and started brushing snow from the windows, going from front to back, finishing at the windshield on the passenger side. As I swept my brush across it, Sam's face appeared. He looked up at me and smiled. With uncharacteristic spontaneity I made a silly face, and he laughed. Our eyes met, and I hurriedly looked away. Then I finished up, hopped in the front seat, and maneuvered the car into the alley.

CHAPTER 20

I HAD A NEW SISTER, and when she was two weeks old I headed to the farm to make her acquaintance. She had been given the names Frances Margaret Grace–Frannie, for short. Richard, a big fan of the British royal family, had insisted on the aristocratic string of names.

At the farm I found my mother and Richard bleary-eyed and weary, yet seemingly happy. Richard was the most affable and relaxed that I had ever seen him. He had taken some time off work to look after the animals while my mother shuffled around in her bathrobe, tending to my little sister–feeding, bathing, changing diapers. In between Frannie lay in her crib sound asleep with her arms raised up next to her head, fists clenched like a little activist.

I stayed for two nights, then took my leave and headed back to Toronto.

The incident at The Freehouse occupied my thoughts as I drove. Now that I was heading back there I needed to understand what had happened. I had definitely seen that light … but what did it mean? Was I *attracted* to Sam? Hardly–he wasn't my type. He didn't own a flashy car, was not sophisticated or urbane … he wasn't even that good looking, with short-cropped blonde hair, a rather large nose, and eyes that were set just a little too close together. I had always liked tall men, but Sam was only a couple of inches taller than me. Besides, we had never had any chemistry, so it made no sense. But then … a lot of things made no sense. Like the fact that I couldn't walk down the street in broad daylight without being besieged by anxiety. Or that I couldn't have normal friendships with people. It made no sense that I only felt safe if I isolated myself, or that I saw no future, or that I could no longer buy clothes because I had no sense of who I was or what I liked. So many things made no sense.

But–okay. If I for the moment assumed that I *was* attracted to Sam … nothing would happen anyway because he had a girlfriend he was crazy about. Plus, I couldn't do relationships. Of any kind. So I should put it out of my mind and stop obsessing about it.

I should stop it now.

But I couldn't stop it. And as soon as I saw Sam push through the door of The Freehouse the following evening, I knew why. The way he smiled when he saw me, the way the energy in the room suddenly felt heightened when he entered it, proved that something genuine had happened. It had not been my imagination.

The evening passed quickly, and by midnight Sam, who was on manager duty, had let both Jordan and Leila go home, leaving just the two of us working. The last customers staggered out a few minutes past 1 a.m. and Sam deftly locked the door behind them, spun around, and beamed a smile at me. "Do you want a drink?"

I agreed to a glass of wine, and he fetched a beer for himself. Then he sat down opposite me at the table where I was busy cashing out. My nerves tingled, and it took all the strength I had to focus on the counting and my calculations. When I finished I pushed the float towards him and we both took awkward sips of our drinks. There was an energy around us that I found both terrifying and exhilarating.

We spoke at the same time: "I always meant to ask you …" "So how is it …?"

We both smiled.

"You go ahead," I said quickly.

"No ... you first," he said.

I drew in a breath. "I was just going to ask how your band is doing these days ... are you getting any gigs?"

"No, but we're rehearsing a lot," he said, "I don't think we're quite ready to play live yet. Soon. Another two or three months."

"What kind of music do you play?" I hoped I didn't sound too forced.

"Kind of British new wave. I'm really into Roxy Music, I love their sound. And the Simple Minds. Do you know them?"

I shook my head, feeling ignorant. I didn't listen to the radio, and never went to clubs where new music was being played. My current musical obsession was Joni Mitchell, whom I had discovered when CJ brought in a cassette tape of her latest album and played it at work. I found that her lyrics spoke to me with amazing clarity–what a revelation that I was not alone in my emotional wasteland, that someone had gone before me and had made it through. Since then, I had bought nearly all her albums, and studied her lyrics like a sleuth searching for clues. It gave me hope that I, too, might find my way to the light one day.

"They're a British band. I saw them perform last year and was blown away. Their lead singer wears all this heavy makeup and has a really dark sound, but their songs are all about beauty, truth, and transcendence."

"I'll have to check them out," I said, and meant it. Beauty, truth, transcendence–sign me up!

He grinned and took a sip of his beer. "So ... my question: what are you doing in Toronto?"

"I ... um ... just waitressing," I said, tripping over the words.

He laughed like I had made a funny joke. "No one comes to Toronto just for that."

It was true, of course. People came to Toronto to be actors, models, artists, musicians. To be discovered. To find validation from outside. To fix their brokenness.

"I guess I hoped to find out when I got here," I said.

"And are you finding out?"

"... Maybe."

I did not mean to sound coy; I just wasn't sure what to say. Should I tell him the truth–that I was a lost little bunny, flailing around in my own neuroses, with no sense of direction? I'd only just sat down with him. Yet he was looking at me with such earnestness that I suddenly felt a powerful need to remove my mask. I took a deep breath.

"I'm ... kinda in the midst of a meltdown," I said.

There was the tiniest pause, as though he was ever-so-slightly discomfited. "Oh!" he said, "I would not have guessed. You don't ... seem like that."

"Like what?"

He grimaced. "Sorry, that didn't come out right. I just mean that you seem like the kind of person who has it all very much together."

I grinned. "Yeah, well. Sometimes the people who seem to have their shit together the most are the biggest nut jobs. They're just good at acting."

"Ah, so you came here to be an actress!"

We both laughed.

"Everyone puts on an act to some degree, though, don't you think?" he continued. "It's rare to meet people who are truly genuine. Most people try to hide who they are."

I was mildly amazed at how fast we had reached this depth. I could not remember the last time I had talked to someone like this, about something that really mattered. "But to be genuine you first have to know who you are," I said. "Most of us are fixed into a mould, and a lot of the time we don't even know what happened to make us the way we are–we can't separate our conditioning from the objective reality. We act in ways that are automatic because that's what we've been programmed to do. Breaking free so that we're not automatons is pretty much the hardest thing there is."

He stared at me, and suddenly I felt incredibly self-conscious. What a ridiculous outburst–he probably thought I was insane. Or worse, a total deadbeat.

"It's the biggest challenge in every person's life, I think," he said.

I exhaled. He seemed to get it. "Well," I said, "that's what I'm doing in Toronto."

He regarded me for a moment, then slowly smiled.

We talked. Our conversation came without effort, one topic flowing into the next. Soon I had shared with him things I had never expected to share, like that I was seeing a psychiatrist, and that I was sifting through my past to get some clarity. I told him that my parents had split when I was five, that my mother had travelled to Canada to help out Klara and taken me with her, that we'd gone to Cyprus, then back to Iceland, then to Canada again. I told him I'd moved out–"or, actually my mother and her husband moved out"–when I was sixteen, and that I'd been living on my own since then. I told him about the house I owned, and how I came to own it. I told him about Richard's endless rules and insane need for control. I told him that he and my mother had just had a baby, and that I'd been at their farm a couple of days ago, meeting my little sister.

He listened intently, and for the first time in a very, very long time I felt that someone truly heard me.

Into my reminiscences he weaved his own story. He had gone through a rough time when he finished high school; had left town and gone out West to plant trees. I was aware that this was something people did when they didn't know what else to do–unskilled labour that paid a decent amount of money. He had only been back in Toronto for a few months, and his dad had helped him out by giving him this job. He didn't get along with his dad, but he had to pay his rent, and working these few shifts at the restaurant allowed him to focus on what he really loved: making music. He told me that his parents had been together since they were teenagers, that his mother was an amazing person, and that he thought his dad was having an affair with his secretary. When he told me the last part he gripped the handle of his beer mug so tightly that his knuckles went white.

Time flew, and when I happened to glance at my watch it was 3 a.m. I started–I had an appointment with Dr. Diamond in the morning and needed to get some rest. "I have to go," I said abruptly, "I need to get up early."

"What are you doing tomorrow night?" he asked, not missing a beat.

I tensed. Despite our wonderful rapport I had not expected that. Surely he was not suggesting we go on a *date* … what about his girlfriend?

"Meet me," he added quickly, his voice soft. "Let's have dinner or something."

I grimaced inwardly. *Men.* "What about Sylvie?"

He looked momentarily confused. "Sylvie?" He shook his head. "We broke up, like, a month ago."

"Oh!" I said, sounding more flustered than I meant to. "But … I thought you guys were so committed."

"Well, we were–until we weren't."

I started gathering up my stuff, my thoughts suddenly a jumble of confusion.

"So …" he said, leaning forward and looking at me expectantly, "can we see each other tomorrow? I would love to keep talking."

I knew what he meant. I felt the same. Rather than exhausting our conversation, I felt like each topic opened up a new one. We had only been sitting there for a couple of hours, yet I felt like we could talk the rest of our lives and never run out of things to say. But going on a date was inconceivable. I had already tried dating in my compromised state–a guy I had met in the laundromat and had dinner with a few times–and it had not gone well. Being out with him had always brought on a torrent of excruciatingly bad feelings that I could not really define, so I had ended it.

"I can't. I have plans. I'm sorry," I lied. My only plans were to stay bunkered inside my apartment, listening to Joni Mitchell records and writing in my journal.

"Ah, okay," he said breezily, but I could tell he was disappointed.

"You're working Wednesday, right?" I asked.

"Yep."

"I'll see you then."

Wednesday came, and the energy connecting us was palpable. I could tell that Sam wanted to be alone with me and sure enough he hustled both Jordan and Leila out the door well before closing time, even finishing up Jordan's tasks in the dining room so he could leave early. We sat at the same table as before; he got us drinks; I finished my cashing out; then we resumed our conversation almost like we were picking up from where we had left off, four nights earlier.

He mentioned that Sylvie had been over at his place earlier that day, picking up the remainder of her stuff.

"What happened with her?" I ventured. "You seemed so happy."

He grimaced. "Yeah. Honestly? I don't know what happened. I lost myself. I became this 'yes' guy, agreeing to everything even though it wasn't what I wanted. I felt forced to do things I didn't really want to do. A couple of months after we started seeing each other my roommate moved out and I needed someone to help pay the rent, so Sylvie said, 'why don't I move in' and I just … agreed, even though I knew in my heart that it wasn't a good idea. A week later she had rearranged everything in the apartment, and two weeks after that she and her mother were planning our wedding. I'm serious!" he exclaimed when I started laughing. "Honest to God, they were planning our wedding. It was too much. So I told her I didn't want to get married, I didn't want to get a new couch, I didn't want to get cable for the TV, and I didn't want to be told how to fold the towels. She got really upset and moved out."

"I'm sorry," I said, "I didn't mean to laugh. It just sounds so crazy."

"It *was* crazy. I don't know what happened–it's like I stopped having a mind of my own, I let her take over, and I lied to myself that I was okay with it. And the more I lied to myself, the weaker I got."

"But you stopped it in the end," I said.

"Yeah. I did. And I don't want to ever go there again. I've made a pact with myself that I won't have another dishonest relationship like that. I'd rather be alone than in a relationship where I can't be myself–where I have to make myself fit into a mould that someone else has made."

I nodded. "I get that."

"What about you?" he said, after a beat. "What's your story? Are you single, or seeing someone, or …?"

"No," I said quickly, "not seeing anyone".

He waited for me to say more, so I told him about Shane. About how we had moved to Toronto together, how I started to feel insecure and weak around him, how I had broken it off. "I lost myself too, though my story isn't the same as yours. The only good thing to come out of that relationship was that I started to see a shrink. And I've since realised that Shane was not the problem–the problem was me, and I have to fix me before I do anything else."

He nodded, waiting.

"I have to go back, pick everything apart and try to figure out what really happened. Try to make connections between past events and the way I am acting today. Most of the time I'm reacting to old stuff that has nothing to do with here-and-now, but I can't really see what is what. I have to get clear. I have to get my mental vision back. I want to be free from things in the past that are controlling me."

"You're looking for the truth," he said.

The way he said it was so simple that I looked at him in wonder.

"What you're doing is rare," he said matter-of-factly. "I admire that."

"Thanks," I said.

He touched the back of my hand with the tips of his fingers. I had not expected it, and instinctively recoiled. He withdrew his hand hastily, like he'd burned it.

"I'm sorry," I said, "I just ..."

"No, I'm sorry," he said, "I don't want to make you uncomfortable. I just love talking to you."

"I love talking to you, too," I blurted, "but I can't handle anything more than that right now. I'm going through a really tough time. I can't have a relationship with anyone."

There. It was out. I felt a swell of relief. I had to be honest with him; it was impossible not to be.

"Sure," he said, striving to keep his voice light, "I understand."

"It's nothing to do with you, it's ..."

"Nah, it's fine," he said. He grinned, but something had settled over him–an affectation; an armour. It threw me. I hated that I had rebuffed him, hated that he was now embarrassed because of me.

"I would really love it if we could be friends," I said, and I meant it. In the year and a half that I had lived in Toronto I had made numerous acquaintances but no friends. I had kept people at arm's length, had not felt a connection with anyone, or trusted anyone, or both. Now, for the first time, I thought about how good it would be to have a friend. To have Sam as a friend.

"Yeah! Yeah, of course," he said hastily. "Me too."

There was an awkward silence, in which we both averted our eyes.

"I should probably go," I said.

"Yeah," he said, getting to his feet. "I need to get home too."

We locked up without speaking, and he walked me to my car.

"Can I give you a ride home?" I offered.

"Nah, I'll walk. It's not far."

"Okay, then."

"Okay."

I got in my car, and sat watching him as he ambled up the alley, collar turned up, hands in his pockets, slightly stooped.

CHAPTER 21

And so, Sam and I became friends. We sought each other out after work and talked long into the night, both of us deriving nourishment from being in each other's company. He, too, had experienced spiritual amnesia and blindness–that rough time he alluded to the first night we sat down and really talked. It had been a dark period in his life, he said, when he lost all perspective and drifted through the days, disconnected and lost. He told me about how his dad threw him out of the house, and how he started doing drugs to numb himself.

"Why did your dad throw you out?"

"I went berserk one night and smashed his liquor cabinet. I found out he was cheating on my mother and I hated him for it.

She gave up everything for him–for us. She is a nurse, and when he was seriously ill with meningitis she quit her job so she could be by his side until he recovered. Whenever any of us are in trouble, or sick, or even just feeling depressed–she's there. She's the strongest person I know. But then, that's what mothers do. They're there for you. They're amazing."

Was that what mothers did?

"Tell me how you found your way out of all that," I said, leaning against the side of the booth in which we were sitting, needing his story, to know how he had come through it.

While he was out West planting trees he had thought a lot–about life, about God. Something gentle and benign had forced its way through the pain and rage he felt. "It's hard to explain, but I started to look at what I'd had in my childhood, as opposed to what I had *not* had, and slowly I started to become grateful. I met a lot of people out West who'd had really shitty childhoods–parents who were drug addicts, or alcoholics, or mentally disturbed. These people were lost and confused, and you could really see how all the shit they'd experienced was causing them to destroy themselves with substance abuse–or with their own anger or self-hate. Unless they underwent a radical change, they didn't stand a chance. And I started thinking about what it was that made some people go through these radical changes, while others were unable to find their way. Why did most people just keep digging themselves deeper and deeper into a hole they were always trying to climb out of? And why did others find some kind of …" he paused, searched for the word, "… grace? Something that allowed them to *see* and to transcend their past."

As I listened to him it felt like every cell of my body that had previously been clenched gently unfolded and opened. His words edified me. I was like a parched traveller who had just come upon a stream of fresh water. I needed to drink, and drink, and then drink some more.

"Eventually I came back here and patched things up with my dad. I decided I wanted to live in the light. I wanted to create. I wanted to do good. And I never wanted to go back to that place again, of endless resentment and self-pity and self-deception." He paused. "And then I met you. You want to break free. You want to live in the truth. And … I see a light in you. I see that grace. It's so rare."

A light. He saw a light in me. Just as I had seen a light in him.

"That's good," I said softly. "Thank you."

I felt like a loser for not going to university, yet the fact was that I was getting an education with Dr. Diamond that felt like the most important thing I could possibly learn. In examining my own psyche, I was learning so much about what it meant to be human. On the road to maturity there are many successive stages, Dr. Diamond explained, and we must integrate each before moving on to the next. No one ever passes through all the stages perfectly–everyone's life is marred by disappointment, pain, trauma. As humans, we are wired to avoid those things–we shrink from them and seek to numb ourselves in an effort to survive. We shut down feelings and instincts that would otherwise guide us to become who we are meant to be. So if we are to be whole again we must go back, feel the feelings we numbed, move through our transitions, and build our lives on a new, conscious foundation.

"Yes!" Sam exclaimed when I told him all this, "I remember seeing a TV program about how some people learn to walk before they can crawl, and because they miss that stage–the crawling stage–they have to go back and learn it manually."

I grinned. "I'm learning to crawl right now."

He opened his mouth as though he wanted to say something, but stopped.

"What?" I said playfully.

His face grew serious. "Do you think …"

I braced myself. I knew what he wanted to say.

"Do you think this can ever be … something more?"

I inhaled deeply. How could I tell him that I wanted that more than anything else? The tenderness I felt for, and with, Sam had me captivated. I thought of him constantly, and all the things we talked about. He helped me to see myself. I had never viewed my sessions with Dr. Diamond as a search for truth, but of course that was precisely what they were. I was peeling back the things I had not had the capacity to face before, seeking what I had truly felt before I went numb. My struggle was common to all people who yearned to cast off the shackles and walk strong. We were a tribe, those of us who thirsted for truth, who craved freedom. Some people were content to spend their lives in half-lit, half-alive places. Some were even content to live their lives in complete darkness, ruled by a force of which they were not conscious, marionettes to a sinister puppet master. I would not be one of those people. Sam was not one of those people. I knew I loved him. I longed to see him outside of work, to build a proper relationship–go to the movies and then out for a drink; cook dinner together and then make love; get fresh bagels on a Saturday morning and have brunch at the kitchen table while reading the paper and discussing current affairs and politics. An easy, uncomplicated life; a normal life.

Yet somewhere deep inside me a sinister voice whispered that such a life was meant for others, not for me. Never for me. I was trapped; beholden to a demon that resided inside me and would not let me walk free.

"I don't want anything from you," he said gently. "I just want to be with you. Just … to spend time. Whatever you feel prepared to give."

"What I said to you before," I began, "you know, when we first talked about this … it wasn't a rejection of you. I know that … *this*, what we've found, it's … different. In the sense that I have to bring all of myself. I want to bring *all* of myself. There's no hiding behind a façade this time. But there are parts of my own self that I don't even have access to. Parts that feel like they've been taken over by someone–or something–else." I paused. "I'm trying to move beyond that. I'm trying really hard. I'm constantly thinking about how I can do that, how I can be free to …" I wanted to say *love*, but stopped myself–too sappy. "… To be with someone."

"If you *were* free," he said, and I could see the effort it took for him to speak, "… do you think you might want … this?"

"Yes!" I said a little too eagerly. "Yes. That's the reason I am doing all this work. To feel alive again. To be ready for … something like this."

Tentatively he reached out and took my hand.

"Maybe," I said, my voice tight, "… maybe if we plant this little seed, and give it some shelter, it can grow."

He pressed my hand, then shifted around until he was next to me. Hesitating for a moment he leaned towards me, met my eyes, and we kissed.

Thus began our love affair, our perfect meeting of souls. We both felt that we had found something pure and extraordinary. We spoke of it often, and felt humbled by it. Yet even after we had declared our love for one another, Sam and I continued to meet only after our shifts at The Freehouse. I insisted we keep it that way, and that our relationship remain a secret. The prospect of revealing it to the outside world terrified me–at the time I didn't know why, but now I think I understand: every time I had felt genuine love in my life, that fragile feeling had been shattered by external forces, and the relationship had not been sustained.

Yet there was something else, too. The stronger my feelings for

Sam became, the more brutal was the inner ravaging. It was as though a force, an entity, had taken up residence in me, its sole purpose being to destroy anything that made me feel alive. The more I pulled towards the light, the greater the hold exerted by this force, like a hand at the bottom of a well that pulled me down as I frantically tried to free myself. The greater my desperation, the stronger its power over me. This force was inside me ... yet it was not *of* me. I felt possessed by it, *owned* by it, but it was not the real me. "It" was my jailer.

I grew obsessed with trying to break free, consumed with trying to find out why I could not be normal, why I felt such abject self-hatred. Dr. Diamond–my steadfast guide on this relentless quest–felt that we needed to discover an incident, or a series of incidents, that were at the root of my self-sabotage. He had begun to suspect sexual trauma or molestation so terrible that I had blocked it from my conscious memory. All the evidence seemed to point to it: shame; fear of intimacy; terror of commitment, of losing myself in a relationship, of being annihilated.

I took to walking the streets of the city–usually at night, because daylight made me feel too exposed. I needed to move my body, to seek release from the turbulence within. As I walked, I thought and thought; returning home, I wrote and wrote. I mined my subconscious for answers, turning the events of my life over, and then over again–examining them, searching for revelations, explanations, solutions. I was so uncompromising, so grimly determined, that both Dr. Diamond and Sam urged me to ease up, to take a break, or I might compromise my health. But I couldn't. There was no "break" from the voice in my head that whispered incessantly that I was *all wrong*, that doused me in shame and drove me to isolate inside my small apartment because I felt like every person that glanced at me on the street had the power to destroy me.

I ached to feel a part of life. On one occasion, frantically needing to prove that I could do the things ordinary people did, I agreed to have dinner with Sam in a restaurant. We met at a glossy venue on Parliament Street called Lipstick. He was already there when I arrived, and as soon as I sat down opposite him I felt the crush of self-erasure. Desperately I tried to appear normal as I talked to Sam and the waiter, fighting to stay in control, to push away the beast that was pulling me down into the murky depths. The next hour and a half were an exhausting struggle to keep the monster at bay–to keep it from overwhelming me.

Somehow I got through dinner, then said I had to leave. Sam walked me to the subway stop and offered to accompany me home. I declined, and felt nothing but relief when I was on the subway, alone, for only then did the inner ravaging stop. Nonetheless I felt excruciating defeat at having failed to bridge the chasm between us, and to be normal. Everything seemed hopeless, and the conviction that I was a fundamentally flawed person who could never be intimate with another human being burned inside of me.

While I obsessed about finding the key to unlock my prison, Sam saw the bigger picture. One night after our shift, sitting at the table that I had begun to think of as ours, I tried to explain that I felt like there were two forces at war inside me, caught in a ferocious battle. "It's like being in the fires of hell."

"That's because it is the fires of hell," Sam said. "Heaven and hell are inside of us. Good and evil are fighting for possession of you, and the darkness ravages you precisely because you're so committed to finding the truth. Resist it!"

I stared at him. What would I do without his insight? When I saw my struggle through his eyes, it gained new meaning. I was not just some neurotic dumbass, but a warrior fighting the darkness so that I could be born into the light. I no longer wanted to live in a state of numbness, to be half-alive. I wanted to *feel.* I wanted to be moved. I wanted to laugh, cry, feel connected to other people. I wanted *myself.*

CHAPTER 22

It was new, this faith Sam had in me, this being seen. I had found shelter and wanted only to rest a while. My greatest fear was that "it" would emerge from the depths and, like a serpent, strike–killing this tender thing that I had found, this love that was like a tiny bud with its own, delicate life. "It can't," Sam said with emphasis when I told him of my fear. "Nothing can touch this. It's stronger than that." I listened, took comfort, yet deep down I knew how fragile it was, that any sudden movement might cause it to shatter.

"Do you think you might just need time to trust me?" Sam said hesitantly one night when we had finished closing up. We had been meeting after work for nearly four months. I could sense his resolve waning, his frustration building. He wanted more. He wanted me as his partner. He had become my best friend and my staunchest ally, yet … how could he have a proper relationship with someone as damaged as me? "I don't want anything from you, I just want us to be together," he would say and, miserably, I would reply: "I know."

There was no way I could convey to him the strength of the toxic energy that kept me isolated, or my terror that it would snuff out the tiny flame that now burned between us. I did not know where that energy came from, and Dr. Diamond was at a loss. Plenty of things in my life had gone wrong, yet none of them seemed to warrant this extreme self-erasure, this self-sabotage. He continued to believe that I had been the victim of something so traumatic that my conscious mind could not admit it, and he began to suggest hypnosis as a potential way forward.

One of Sam's band mates was throwing a party. His friends were all going to be there. He mentioned it in passing one Thursday night when we were together, and I knew he wanted me to go with him, though he would not say so. I could see it in his averted gaze, in the subtle flexing of his jaw. I felt the old familiar unease engulf me, and then the revolt: *Why shouldn't I go? Why can't I be normal?*

Fearful, yet driven by a burning frustration, I said I would go. We arranged that I would pick him up and we would drive to the party together.

Getting ready at home beforehand–applying my makeup, getting dressed in my most flattering outfit–I felt a thrumming dread. Driving to Sam's house I struggled to push away the creeping doubts that accosted me. I parked in front of his building and made my way up the steps to a stately front door with a big oval window. My hand trembled a little when I rang the doorbell. Through the bevelled glass I saw light pour forth on the second-floor landing with the opening of a door, and then saw Sam jog easily down the stairs. He pulled open the door, kissed me lightly on the lips, then gestured for me to ascend the stairs ahead of him. I stepped tentatively into his apartment–a place I had pictured in my mind's eye many times. I was in a corridor; to one side was a living room, and next to that a kitchen. I spied a stack of newspapers on the floor next to an old fridge. To my right were two doors–one stood ajar, and I saw it was a bedroom; the other was closed. Looking around shyly, it struck me how absurd it was that Sam and I had spent all those hours together, opened our hearts wide to one another, yet I had never seen these elements of his daily life. I glanced at him; he smiled at me and I smiled back–he must be thinking the same thing, I thought, that it was strange knowing each other's deepest thoughts and feelings and at the same time being completely unfamiliar with the other's day-to-day routines.

I waited as he got his coat; then we went outside to my car. As we drove I felt a dark tension mounting and pushed aside the encroaching notion that I had made a grave mistake–that I should never have let myself believe that I could just go out with the guy I loved, like a normal human being. Now I would have to keep up the gruelling pretence that I was just as sane as the next person, not an emotional invalid. Perhaps I should call the whole thing off, just drop Sam at his friend's place and go back to the safety of my chrysalis. Yet on some level I also knew that this evening was a test–he would not wait forever, and I had to prove to him that I could do this, that there was at least some tiny progression forward.

I parked, and we walked the block or so to where the party was. Sam took my hand and I felt myself grow tense. He had often taken my hand when we were alone–we had kissed, held each other, pressed our bodies together, but somehow this holding hands in public terrified me. I had an impulse to scream, but stifled it.

I would not blow this.

The party was in the basement of a house a couple of blocks west of Yonge Street, south of Bloor. Inside, the only light came from a lamp in the corner, and it took a few moments for my eyes to adjust. People glided past or stood in groups, and the whole experience seemed surreal. I felt horribly conspicuous, certain that anyone who looked at me could see right through to the sickness at my core. Sam, oblivious to my discomposure, led the way to the kitchen, which was filled with people. He introduced me to his friends, his hand touching my lower back, while I smiled and nodded. He was proud of me, I could tell, and I felt like the biggest shit alive because I realised that I didn't want to be there, with him, or any of them. I didn't fit, I didn't belong … *what had possessed me to come here*?

Sam produced a bottle of wine and poured two glasses, handing one to me. Then he squeezed my arm and went off to say hello to someone. I left the kitchen and returned to the dark room, finding a corner in which to stand, grateful for the din of the music that prevented me from having to speak. I recognised it as the Simple Minds' *New Gold Dream* album. Sam had mentioned it during one of our talks as being one of his favourite albums right now. He said it was about faith, and God, and rebirth, and that was enough for me: I had gone out and bought it the very next day. He had been so glad when I told him, and had spoken passionately about music and art that channelled the divine, that served the light. I had listened, enraptured, as he told me how he felt it was the duty of artists to convey the life force–to inspire, edify, offer hope.

I took a swig of my wine. The room was crowded, and someone passed me a joint. I took a toke, then another, and instantly realised what a mistake it was: I had felt self-conscious before, but now I was headed for full-blown paranoia. Sam re-appeared and put his arm around me. "You okay?" he asked, "do you want another drink?" I shook my head. I was starting to panic. I needed to leave.

"I have to get out of here," I told him. "I don't feel good."

He put down his drink. "Okay," he said. "We'll go."

"You stay," I said. It was early and I didn't want to ruin his evening. He shook his head, then took my hand and led me through to the front door.

"Sam, really–you stay," I said again when we were outside.

"No," he said. "This is you and me, going out. I want to be with you."

"Where do you want to go, then?" I said, my voice reedy.

He shrugged. "I'm up for anything."

I took a deep breath. "We could go dancing," I said.

I had wanted to go dancing with him ever since he had come in to The Freehouse one night with Sylvie on their way to a club, both of them stoked to hit the dancefloor. It had become one of our things … "When you are better we can go dancing," he had said, and I had made that thought mine … *yes, when I am better we will dance.*

"Okay!" he said, brightening. "Where?"

I gestured. "Yonge is just over there."

I had never been to a dance club in Toronto, but Sam knew the best ones and led the way to a place that was not far away. It was throbbing with excitement when we arrived, the music loud and pulsating, bodies packed in, bouncing and gyrating. Sam held my hand and headed for the bar, and while we waited to be served I felt a renewed surge of defiant rage: *I will not let my happiness be destroyed;* I will be normal.

"I'll have a shot of tequila," I said to the bartender, and Sam looked at me in surprise. I didn't care. I was going to do what I wanted to this evening. Sam held up two fingers to indicate two shots. The barman brought them, plus lemon slices and a shaker of salt. I went first, shaking salt onto the back of my hand, licking it, downing the tequila, then sucking on the lemon. I looked at Sam–he was laughing, but I thought I saw a hint of concern in his eyes. I ordered two more shots, looking at him, willing him to stop me. He didn't. We repeated the process. I felt the alcohol surge through me, taking control. I grabbed Sam's arm and dragged him onto the dance floor. We began moving in time with the music, then Sam was next to me, grabbing me, pressing me to him. I squirmed away, but he grabbed me again. I pushed him, hard. He stumbled backward, onto a guy behind him. Something had risen up in me, a cold and calculated fury, lifeless and dispassionate. This fury was not directed at anything or anyone in particular; it was simply filling my insides, and now when I looked at Sam I felt only a cold contempt. His stricken face made me want to hurt him even more. I would walk away, leave him standing in his insipid, maudlin pain. Turning, I pushed through the crowd, heading for the exit. Just before I reached it I felt a hand clasp my arm. I spun around, and shook it off with one sharp movement. Sam's face showed confusion, hurt and shock; I felt only derision. Then I heard my own voice–dark, menacing, and low: "*Don't touch me.*"

He stopped. Something shifted behind his eyes and his whole body went slack, as though a fresh realisation had just dawned on him, like he finally understood. I could see him surrender to this new comprehension. In so doing, he let go of me. It was as though he remained standing in one world while I was thrown backward into another, filled with demons and fire and unfathomable shame.

In that moment I knew I had done it. At last, it had happened. This tender thing we had found, that we had been trying to nurture into life for the previous five months, had now been destroyed. "It" had won.

Without thinking I turned and ran down the steps, out onto Yonge Street, with its depraved Saturday night revelry, its roving bands of misfits and partygoers. Sam kept pace with me until we were at my car, and I wondered the whole time why he was there–why he wanted to stay, what his problem was. I had given him ample reason to give up on me–why didn't he just leave?

I unlocked the car and he got into the passenger seat.

I put my hands on the steering wheel and clenched them so hard that my knuckles turned white.

"Talk to me!" he shouted, as though trying to reach me through the stony silence.

I could not speak: I *was* that cold fury now.

He hesitated a moment, looking at me, then got out of the car and slammed the door. I turned the key in the ignition and drove away with a squealing of tires–drunk and messed up and filled with a macabre satisfaction that I had finally managed to destroy the one thing that made me feel alive.

CHAPTER 23

THE NEXT MORNING, I awoke crushed with remorse. My worst fears had materialised: the toxic force within me had won. Those things that Sam and I had found–the tenderness, the beauty, the hope–had all been killed, and I was the executioner. Nothing between us would ever be the same.

I needed my mother; needed her assurance that all would be okay. I had four days off, so on Monday morning, when I knew Richard would be at work during the daytime, I got in my car and drove down to the farm. I needed to pour it all out to her like a confession, to unburden myself of this terrible guilt. We sat out on the small paved veranda in front of her house while my baby sister Frannie lay on a quilt in the grass practicing some early crawling manoeuvres. My mother listened as I told her all about my relationship with Sam and how I felt I had destroyed what we had found. She was quiet for a few moments. I waited for her soothing words of comfort.

"Well," she said at length, "I think maybe it's good for you to have your heart broken. You've broken some hearts too, and now the shoe is on the other foot. It might teach you humility."

I stared straight ahead, not knowing what to think, or say. A part of me wanted to revolt, yet an even stronger part felt that, yes, she was right–this was what I deserved. I needed to be brought down, taught a lesson. I was bad. *Guilty.*

A breeze was starting up, the leaves on the trees rustled. A numbness settled over me, and in that numbness I did feel a modicum of comfort, like I had slipped on an old, worn, familiar pair of slippers. My mother leaned back in her chair and sighed, closing her eyes. In front of us, my little sister moved her legs with great exertion, trying to push herself forward on the blanket, towards us.

As I had expected, things with Sam changed. I did not see him for twelve days, and when he arrived for our next shift together he was late and hastened past the bar without acknowledging me. Throughout the evening he kept to himself at the back of the restaurant, chatting to Jordan, reading the paper. I did what I always did–suppressed my feelings, acted competent, and got through the shift. We did not speak.

When the last customers had gone I went to the front door and locked it, then took a deep breath and walked into the back of the restaurant where he sat, hunched over the Toronto Star travel section.

"Can we talk?" I asked.

He swivelled around to face me, his face ashen.

"I'm so sorry," I said fervently, perching on a chair opposite him. "I was afraid something like that would happen. I just want you to know that … that was not me. Not the real me. That was … *it.*"

He leaned forward and put his elbows on his knees. I could see his mind struggling, gathering thoughts, forming words. At last he said, "I thought I could do this, but I can't. I was hoping things would get better, but …" he raised himself up and looked at me, his eyes so vulnerable that I had to look away.

I had expected this response, but not the pain that suddenly engulfed me.

"I'm sorry," I whispered.

Our eyes met. Then, stiffly, as though the floodgates might break if he moved too fast, he turned back to his paper. I got up, wishing he would reach out then and take hold of my arm, tell me one more time that I would soon get better, that he would wait, that we could make it happen if we just tried hard enough. But deep down I knew I could not force this rebirth. I had to let go, and so did he.

The Freehouse was in decline. Business in the dining room had slowed to a drip, and the jazz band had been let go. The upscale clientele that Joe Brady sought to attract had, over the course of the winter, all but disappeared. Now Frank and his entourage kept the place running, his minions skulking around furtively looking like they were covered in a thin layer of ash. One evening I noticed two of them surreptitiously showing women's suede jackets to customers at the bar–two different colours, mauve and camel. When I asked Leila what they were up to she said the jackets were from a Sears truck that someone in Frank's posse had heisted earlier that day. I was speechless–if not entirely surprised. My first thought was that Joe, the owner, who happened to be dining there that evening, would catch on and there would be some kind of altercation. But a half hour later I spotted Joe in the corner with one of the men, proffering a wad of cash as payment for two jackets.

Amidst the degeneration, Sam and I sidestepped gingerly around one another. The anger and hurt from the night at the dance club gradually softened, and the genuine love we felt for each other broke through like flowers emerging through asphalt. Our bond was strong, we could not let go, and began to meet after hours again, having long conversations into the night. Yet something had changed. I was no longer pretending that I could cross that tempestuous river inside of me to be with him, and I could sense that there were things Sam was not telling me. Soon enough I heard from CJ that he had run into him and Sylvie at the Kensington Market, and when I asked Sam about it, he reluctantly admitted that, yes, he and Sylvie were seeing each other again, and in fact were planning on trying once more to live together.

I was devastated, but had come to accept that I was powerless–I could not insist that he not see her. I saw that he was conflicted, and when I pressed him he admitted that he seemed to lose all resolve when he was with Sylvie, that he really did not know what he was doing. I knew I should probably move on. Yet even with our relationship so altered, the thought of leaving Sam was unbearable. He was my confidant, my best friend, and even in this tangled web, with those forces pulling us apart, there was a thread between us that would not be severed. We were truthful with one other. I still shared with him my journey with Dr. Diamond, and he laid bare his inability to extricate himself from Sylvie. I did not judge him–how could I? We were two absolutely imperfect human beings, who nevertheless held a tiny glow of something pure and perfect between us.

Yet things were growing more and more tainted. Sylvie, suspicious of Sam's late nights, began showing up at The Freehouse just before closing time to escort him home. Meanwhile the atmosphere in the bar went from bad to worse. One evening an incident shook me out of my torpor: one of Frank's boys, who had just been released from jail, turned ugly when I refused to let him run a tab at the bar, picked up a bunch of change, and hurled it at me while yelling obscenities. Next, he climbed onto and over the bar, and I was sure he was coming for me. I rushed to get away, but no–he just wanted his coins back. He was promptly hustled out the door by Frank, who on his return apologised profusely and left me a large tip, but the volatility of the incident, and the proliferation of criminals around me, triggered a reaction. It was time to go.

Sam and I did not work together again. At our last shift with each other, a few days earlier, we had parted in front of The Freehouse–Sam heading home to Sylvie, me heading home to my cocoon–neither of us free. In plain view of everyone he put his arms around me and we kissed passionately. Folks passing by on the sidewalk smiled at our frank, uninhibited ardour, and one woman exclaimed, "Oh to be young and in love!" We looked at each other and grinned, and Sam whispered, "Everyone sees it." Then, almost as though he knew the end was coming, he put his arms around me and whispered: "I will always love you. No matter what happens, that will never change." Holding on to him, I nodded. It was one of those things that did not need to be said. Some things are stronger than darkness, and though it may claim its little victories, it can never destroy what resides in the sacred place of the heart.

CHAPTER 24

THAT AUTUMN, THREE SIGNIFICANT events took place.

First, I made a decision to enrol in part-time study at the University of Toronto. Like a concerned father, Dr. Diamond had kindly but firmly suggested that it might be time for me to do something with my life other than slinging beer in a dingy bar. I agreed wholeheartedly ... but *what,* was the still-unanswered question. I still could not see a place for me in the world–not then, and certainly not 20 or 30 years in the future.

"Was there nothing that you enjoyed doing when you were

younger?" Dr. Diamond probed. "No courses you liked in high school?"

My mind circled back to the guidance counsellor and the aptitude test she had given me. I had wanted to go into acting but was convinced that my mother was against it, and even after she assured me that I had her support, that avenue seemed closed and I did not pursue it.

Dr. Diamond frowned when I told him. "Why would your mother not want that for you?" he asked.

I couldn't explain.

"Well, in any case, she does not have the power to decide what you choose to do with your life. You are an adult now; you make your own choices," he said brightly.

The following week I enrolled in three classes: acting, a literature class with an emphasis on stage plays, and a class titled "Religion in Literature" taught by an elderly Catholic priest with wild, white hair, who delivered thunderous sermons to rapturous audiences, and whose favourite refrain was "You've lost your sense of wonder!" I enjoyed his dramatic tutorials in which he lambasted us, his students, for our sheep-like complacency and lack of original thought. "You are completely blind!" he would bellow, "You cannot even see what is right in front of you!" On one occasion I watched a fellow student break down and cry out: "I want to see! What do I have to do to see?!" To which the old man leaned forward, looked him in the eye, and said with grave emphasis: "You have to suffer."

I missed Sam terribly. I felt bereft, and longed to share with him all I was learning, all I was seeing, and all I was hearing–especially the truths woven into the great works of literature. He would have understood, like I did, and as none of the other students–sheltered as they were–appeared to. But Sam was gone from my life, and I knew nothing of his affairs. I filled the void he had left by clinging to my sessions with Dr. Diamond like they were flotsam on a stormy ocean, hoping for that elusive breakthrough that would propel me to a tranquil shore.

The second major happening of the autumn was that my mother came to visit me. In the two years that I had lived in the city I had visited Kingston, and my mother, every couple of months. Yet she had never made the two-and-a-half-hour drive to Toronto to see me. She was busy, I knew–with the farm, the animals, my baby sister. She and Richard had managed to go away on holiday only once by hiring an agriculture student to take care of the farm for a few days. They had enlisted my help, as well, on that occasion–I had gone down and stayed a long weekend with the student to help her out and ensure she had everything she needed.

It did not occur to me to wonder at this situation. That I should be the one making trips to see my mother and that she would never come to see me seemed completely normal, like a law of nature that I did not question. This even though I had been struggling mentally and she knew it–after all, I had on more than one occasion phoned her, desperate for support. She had not been curious to see how I lived, where I worked, or what I was up to on a daily basis–to say nothing of wanting to offer protection and comfort. I recalled Sam speaking about his mother–how she was always there for her children, always selfless; how she made sacrifices. My mother, it seemed to me now, had made precious few sacrifices for me.

But that autumn, she and Klara came up for a weekend visit. They stayed with me in my small apartment and we did touristy things like visiting the CN Tower, going out for dinners, catching a concert. I had seen Klara in Toronto a few times when she and Jim were passing through, but had never had the pleasure of showing my mother my surroundings. She took them in with her customary detachment, displaying minimal enthusiasm. Looking back on it now, I see that this visit was a milestone. It forced my mother to acknowledge that I had a whole existence entirely separate from hers. That visit was the beginning of the watershed to come.

The third meaningful event that autumn was that my grandparents extended an invitation for me to come to Iceland for the Christmas holidays.

I had not been back to my native country for more than two years–the last time had been when Vera and I argued and my illusion that I could rely on my father for inclusion and support had shattered. Since then, I had not felt a need to go back–I'd had my hands rather full with my fragile emotional condition. There was no longer an earmarked fund to pay for my flight tickets, and in those days air travel was expensive. Yet when I received the invitation, via letter, from my grandparents, I was profoundly touched. They were not wealthy people, yet they were willing to give me this costly gift. I decided to go.

I do not remember how I told my mother of my decision to spend Christmas in Iceland. I do recall that I drove down to Kingston a few days before I was to leave, to drop off some presents and wish everyone a Merry Christmas. It was a Friday, and my mother and Richard were attending a Christmas dinner and ball at the Royal Military College that evening, while Klara looked after Frannie. I was planning to spend the night at Klara and Jim's, and the following day head out to the farm for a visit with my mother.

I arrived in the late afternoon, and helped Klara get dinner ready. Klara, Jim, my two cousins and I had just sat down to eat when my mother and Richard burst in, a little later than anticipated–she in a long, red ballgown, he in full military regalia. Klara got up and took Frannie from my mother, settling her in a high chair as they quickly reviewed basic instructions for her care.

Somewhat to my surprise, my mother did not greet me when she arrived. As she bustled around, it began to seem like she was wilfully ignoring me. I put it down to the fact that they were late and she was stressed out … yet that could not sufficiently explain the hostility I was picking up from her. I was confused. Was she really giving me the cold shoulder?

Then came a knowing, a small whisper inside me: *You are not crazy.*

I sat perfectly still, and suddenly a new realm of awareness seemed to open up. I saw myself as though from the outside, surrounded by a toxic mist, and I realised that this was not something new, or specific to this moment–it had been there a long time but I had not noticed it. I had breathed it in, absorbed it into my body, allowed it to saturate me at a cellular level. Because of that it had been invisible. But now … for some reason *right now* it could not penetrate. Instead, I saw it there, swirling around the room–not within me, but outside; separate.

Then, as though I was watching a movie, I saw what was going on. My mother was angry because I was leaving to spend Christmas with my Icelandic family. This was my punishment–this excommunication. I was being treated like I was not there, as if I didn't exist. As though I was nothing.

"We're late for God's sake, dahling!" Richard called irritably from the foyer. My mother went to Frannie in her high chair and kissed her. Then, as she passed, she gave me a perfunctory peck on the cheek, devoid of warmth or affection–as though it was her duty. Then she was gone.

I sat motionless, struggling to comprehend. Klara was feeding Frannie, Jim was reading his copy of Scientific American, Sara was claiming to have found a fly in her salad, Billy was looking on. Thoughts roiled furiously through my mind: had no one noticed that my mother had barely acknowledged my presence? Was I crazy to think this was abnormal? *Was* it abnormal? Had the coldness I sensed really been there, or had I imagined it? Was any of this real?

I shut my eyes. I felt both extremely calm and extremely upset. I knew I had to leave before this budding *something* that I didn't yet have a handle on became submerged in confusion and disorientation. I stood up carefully, took my plate and glass into the kitchen, then hesitated a moment before going back into the dining room.

"Thank you so much for dinner," I said, "I think I'm going to leave … I need to get back to Toronto."

Klara and Jim both looked up at the same time. "I thought you were staying for the weekend," Klara said, surprised.

"I need to get back," I said again, "I'm sorry."

"But it's almost eight o'clock, you'll be driving in the dark!"

"That's okay."

Our eyes met. Klara stood up. "Are you sure?"

I nodded, then gave them all a hug goodbye. My overnight bag lay next to the front door and I grabbed it on my way out, then rushed down the porch steps and to my car, as though some strange and unknown force might grab me and pull me back at any moment. As soon as I was on the highway I felt a crazy, wild, irrational sense of freedom. I found a music station and turned the volume up full blast, shouting at the top of my lungs to the songs I knew. Then, about halfway to Toronto, I went silent. A white-hot fury rose within me. How *dare* my mother treat me with condescension? How *dare* she punish me for going to Iceland to spend Christmas with my family? I agreed to go to Canada with her because she promised me a dog. Had she ever intended to make good on it? That dog had been a dangling carrot, used to control me–one that I chased after like a dimwitted puppy. She had used my greatest vulnerability against me, then turned around and stabbed me in the back.

Why had everyone acted like that was perfectly okay?

More to the point: why had *I* acted like it was okay?

I knew the answer to the latter question: because facing the truth was too dangerous. My survival had depended on not upsetting my mother–not contradicting her, not expressing my anger, not owning my feelings. She took any assertion of my independence as a personal affront. Opposing her, in whatever form, meant incurring her wrath. If she cast me off, I had no one.

I had to erase myself to survive.

She had taken me to Canada, not because it was best for me, but because it was good for her. Then, when it suited her to leave me behind, she did. When I was lost, confused and forlorn in a big metropolis, she had not come to my aid. And now *she* was angry with *me* for going to see the family I had left behind when I agreed to become her sidekick?

Driving along Highway 401 at 100 km per hour, I leaned back in the seat and screamed as loud as I could.

It was late when I parked my car in the underground garage of my building and took the elevator up to the womb-like safety of my apartment. I got undressed and lay on my unfurled futon, staring at the sky through the big window on the opposite wall. Clouds raced, covering and uncovering the moon; I felt agitated, as though something way deep in my subconscious was clamouring to emerge. At length I fell asleep and slept fitfully, waking to sunlight streaming in. There was a feeling in my body like a hangover, even though I'd not imbibed a drop of alcohol the previous night. I sensed a change in me, an irrevocable *something* that I could ill define. Anger? Yes–I was angry. That elusive feeling that Dr. Diamond had so often asked me about, which I had never been able to access. But last night on that drive back to Toronto it had erupted, transforming my psyche into a hurricane, flinging bits of life and self around so furiously that I not been able to hold on to a single thought.

My mother. What was she thinking now? She would have gone to pick up Frannie at Klara's and been told that I had left abruptly ... would she wonder why? Undoubtedly–she and Klara would have examined my behaviour from every angle, looking for reasons why I was so "difficult". They would blame my unstable condition–after all, I was the one with the emotional issues, the one forced to see a shrink.

I felt a stab of fury, sharp and sudden, like a flame from a blowtorch. I got out of bed, went to the bathroom, brushed my teeth. Sat on a chair, stood, paced. Stopped, stared at the telephone. What was she doing now? It was 10 a.m. and she would have been up for a few hours. Did she want to talk? Was she sorry that things were not right between us? If I told her how I felt, would she understand?

My heart began to race. I needed to speak to her. Why did I feel this blind terror? It was an old terror, I told myself, the terror of being abandoned if I dared speak my mind. But I did not need to stay silent now. I could survive on my own. I had been surviving on my own for more than four years. I had to remember that.

I no longer needed to disappear in order to live.

Still, what right did I have to say what I needed to say? She was my mother. She had done her duty and made sure my physical needs were taken care of. Was I judging her, overreacting; did I have it all wrong? My grasp on reality was like the moon through my window last night–one moment sharp and clear, the next vague and veiled by clouds.

I did not know what was real any more.

Except that, somewhere … I did.

I wondered what Sam would say if I told him all this. Sam, who was probably lying in bed with Sylvie right now, or out getting bagels so they could read the newspaper together at the kitchen table, in perfect harmony–living the life that I yearned for, with him.

Listen to the voice that speaks the truth. That is probably what he would say.

Swiftly I picked up the phone and began to dial my mother's number, then quickly pressed the switchhook, my heart hammering against my ribcage.

No! I was not crazy. My mother had treated me with icy

detachment last night. She had made it clear that I was banished from the mothership, and I knew, *I knew*, that if I did not find my voice I would be doomed to float around in the vast coldness of space forever–never belonging, never part of this life on Earth.

I dialled, my ears ringing with the blood coursing through me. She picked up on the fourth ring. Her voice was neutral. "Hello?"

"It's me. I need to tell you something."

I had hoped to speak calmly, rationally, intelligently, but instead it spilled out of me like toxic waste, shrill and incoherent. All the stuff: her taking me to Canada because *she* wanted me with her, the broken promise of the dog, her dropping me when she no longer needed me, and now her punitive coldness because I was going back for Christmas. I talked fast, so fast that she could not interject, for I knew that even a dash of her razor-sharp scorn had the power to erase all my convictions.

When I had finished, I slammed the phone down, trembling violently.

Instantly I was afraid that she would call back, that any second the phone would ring and I would be compelled to pick up. She would scream her scathing vitriol at me, and everything I knew, everything I *was*, would be extinguished.

With one swift motion I reached over and pulled the phone jack out of the wall.

It was Saturday, and I had a few last-minute errands to run before my trip the following Tuesday. As I went about my day it struck me that, even though I felt frail, my fear of my surroundings and other people had lessened. I moved with greater confidence, held my head higher than I had done in a long time, and even managed to look people in the eye. I had spoken my truth, and survived. What a remarkable, incredible thing.

But as the day wore on, a creeping sense of guilt came up behind me, lassoing my thoughts. How could I have *said* those things–hurt my mother so? I had not meant to say them. I did not even really believe they were real. Was she feeling awful, too? Was she trying to get in touch with me? Calling and calling my phone that was unplugged back in my apartment? Maybe she wanted to talk, or explain. I hadn't even given her a chance. What a heartless, inconsiderate daughter I was.

I nearly ran back home. The moment I entered my apartment I flew to the phone jack and plugged it back into the wall, then stood up abruptly and backed away, staring at the cord snaking across the floor, expecting the telephone to ring at any moment.

It did not ring. Not that day, nor the next day, nor the day after that.

And then, it was time to go to Iceland.

PART III

Within be fed, without be rich no more.
So shalt thou feed on Death, that feeds on men,
And, Death once dead, there's no more dying then.

-— William Shakespeare, Sonnet 146

CHAPTER 25

Góðir farþegar, velkomin heim.

As the aircraft touched down at Keflavík airport, the mellifluous voice of the Icelandair flight attendant welcomed me home. The low, utilitarian airport terminal, rigged up by the United States military during World War II, hugged the ground amidst the moonscape-like surroundings of the Reykjanes peninsula. It was just past six a.m. and the inky darkness was calm and watchful over the land. Once inside the terminal building I waited for my bag with nervous apprehension, not knowing exactly what I would say to my father. He had written to say that he would prefer it if I did not stay with him and Vera. Their relationship was still under strain and my presence there, he said, would add more pressure. I knew what he was saying: he did not want a repeat of what had happened the last time, when Vera and I clashed. I got that. Nevertheless, it stung.

He stood on the other side of a glass wall, smiling and waving, with scores of others who were there to pick up loved ones. I waved back, happy to see him, reflecting that this was the longest consecutive length of time that I had not seen my father. Two and a half years, during which a lifetime had been undone.

Driving into town, snow-covered lava formations flanking the highway, he asked how I was feeling, and if psychotherapy was helping me. I said that yes, it was. He said that was good. Our exchange was stilted–how much, after all, could I tell him? My entire existence had been turned on its head, and I was still in free-fall. He mentioned that he had a good friend who was a therapist and who was willing to see me while I was in Iceland, if needed. I was touched that he had gone to the trouble of arranging this with his friend. My mind flashed back to my interactions with my mother over the last two years, and her curious indifference to my struggle. What a comfort this was.

It was just before eight a.m. when my father pulled up in front of my grandparents' house. Set back from the street and covered in fresh snow, it looked like it belonged on the front of a Christmas card. The building itself was beautifully symmetrical: in the centre a wide staircase led to a small landing that fanned out into two separate stairways, leading to doors on the left and right. In front of each door was a small, curved balcony with rounded concrete banisters, onto which coloured Christmas lights were affixed, shining bright and cheerful out of the early morning darkness. Above the central landing was my grandparents' kitchen, and through the window I could see my grandmother at the sink. She stopped what she was doing, looked out and waved. A moment later she pulled open the front door with a warm smile as my grandfather came up just behind her, ready to welcome me home.

In Iceland, the advent to Christmas is a magical time. The short days are adorned with sunrises and sunsets that last for hours, creating a symphony of colour in a crystal-clear sky. In the evenings, if conditions are right, the northern lights appear to light up the darkness. It is a time of honouring our common heritage; the things that make us a tribe. Friends and family gather to prepare traditional foods that are consumed only at this special time of year. Cultural events abound: concerts, plays, book readings, art exhibitions, stage shows. Christmas lights are everywhere, and a quiet excitement permeates the air. Children are invariably on their best behaviour in the hope that each of the thirteen Icelandic Yule Lads, who come down from the mountains, one per day, in the advent to Christmas Eve, will leave them a gift in their shoe while they are sleeping.

One afternoon, a few days after I arrived, I was helping my grandmother with some baking. The baking of cookies is taken very seriously in the lead-up to Christmas, and in the past Icelandic homemakers measured their domestic merit by the number of varieties they managed to bake before the Yule. As we rolled bits of gingerbread dough into little balls and pressed half a blanched almond into the top of each, my grandmother cautiously broached the subject of my psychotherapy. Until then she and my grandfather had studiously avoided the topic, as if they found it awkward or embarrassing to talk about. Icelandic has a saying: *Að bera ekki tilfinningar sínar á torg*, literally: "One does not parade one's feelings around in the town square," and this was the prevailing sentiment among my grandparents' generation. Though seeking psychiatric help was slowly becoming more accepted in Iceland, it was still regarded as suspect. My grandparents' notion of it was derived primarily from the TV show Dallas where, according to my grandmother, "Sue Ellen can't even make the smallest decision without first running to see her shrink!" I understood that my grandmother's concern was that, like Sue Ellen, I would lose all autonomy and become entirely dependent on Dr. Diamond. I assured her that the goal was to foster independence and strength so that I could stand on my own.

She was quiet for a few moments and then said: "It was probably hard for you that things didn't work out with your mother and father."

"Yes. It was," I said matter-of-factly.

"We were afraid we would lose you when they split up," she continued. "But then you started coming here after school, and we were so happy that you wanted to spend time with us. We thought maybe that we were helping your mother, too, by giving her the freedom to go out and enjoy herself … perhaps meet someone new. We never wanted to overstep, or offend anyone."

I glanced at her, unsure of what she was trying to say.

She continued, her gaze fixed on the cookies she was forming. "She seemed fine with it at first. It worked out well, you coming here and practicing the piano. You didn't have to go to the day care anymore, which I thought had to be good since it cost money and you didn't seem very happy there. But then … I don't know, at some point she became very cold towards us. But we meant no harm." She paused, and seemed to be struggling with self-recrimination. "Maybe we should have never offered to give you those piano lessons."

"No," I said quickly, eager to appease her discomfort, "*no*, those lessons meant the world to me. I wanted to spend time here. I … this is where I wanted to be."

"It was like she got more and more resentful of us, like she thought we were having too much of an influence on you," she said, then added, "I sometimes wondered if she took you to Canada to get you away from us."

I opened my mouth to utter a platitude, but stopped. Something was reverberating with me, something I could not yet fully grasp.

"Ah, I don't know," she said quickly, standing up from the table and going to the old Rafha stove in the corner to check on the batch of cookies in the oven. "I'm probably just being silly."

We worked in silence for a few moments longer, as I struggled to assign meaning to her remarks. Then she spoke again, and now there was an edge to her voice: "But then, after she met that man, she just … left you. First she takes you all that way, and then just leaves you on your own. Sells the apartment that was supposed to pay for you to come back at least until you were an adult and could decide for yourself where you wanted to live. Even though she bought that house for you, I thought that was wrong."

My kind, forbearing grandmother, whom I never heard speak a disparaging word about anyone–she had seen the very thing that had exploded into my awareness that evening when I drove back to Toronto from Jim and Klara's house. Had *everyone* seen it? Was I the only one who had refused to look at what was right in front of my face? Sitting there at the table, I felt the relief of validation. Others had seen it, too; had felt indignant about it, too. It had not just been me, overreacting. It was real.

A few days before I was scheduled to fly back to Canada, my father and I took a walk together. We had never spoken of how he had experienced his marriage to my mother, though I was of course well aware of my mother's view of him and his alleged treachery. The broad strokes of their relationship I knew: they had met at Bifröst, a business college in West Iceland where both of them lived in dormitories. They fell in love, and became the golden couple on campus–young and beautiful and sprinkled with stardust. My mother was only sixteen, my father nineteen.

About a year into their relationship my mother became pregnant with me. To be unmarried and with child at seventeen-going-on-eighteen was not an anomaly in Iceland at the time, and there was never any question of whether or not they would keep the baby. Yet my mother was adamant that they should get married before I was born, my father said, so they tied the knot in November, a little more than a month before I was ejected from her womb and into the world.

At Bifröst my father had been active in the drama club, and though he secured a good position at a bank after graduating, what he really wanted was to become an actor. There was no formal drama school in Iceland at this time, so he began taking lessons under the auspices of the National Theatre. This motivated my mother to do the same, and she enrolled a year later. They graduated a year apart and my mother's acting career got off to a promising start. She was cast in prominent roles in a couple of large productions, but then the work seemed to dry up for her. At the same time, my father's career was taking off. He had set up a theatre company with some friends, and they were about to embark on a national tour. It was then that my mother decided to go to Canada on the sojourn that was supposed to last just a few weeks, but wound up lasting two years.

"We were not really separated during that time, but not exactly together, either," my father reflected as we strolled along the waterfront in Reykjavík. "It was only supposed to be for a few weeks, but then the two of you just … didn't come back. We were writing to each other and we were still married, but we were unsure of the way forward. She seemed to want a guarantee that everything would be different when the two of you returned. But I couldn't give her that–and neither could she. 'You know how I am, and I can't guarantee that I have changed,' she wrote to me even before she came back to Iceland."

"She told me that you were seeing Erla by then," I said, my mind flashing back to the caustic comments my mother had made about my father's supposed affair with an actress who was on tour with him.

He shook his head. "No. Your mother thought so, but Erla and I did not get involved until you and your mother went to Cyprus, when it seemed highly unlikely that she and I would get back together."

This was new to me. My mother had always claimed that my father had cheated on her, and that had ended their union. That seemed to be the accepted narrative in my mother's family as well–most of them regarded my father as a cheat and a louse.

"I never knew when you were coming back from Cyprus," he continued, "it dragged on and on, with all these false starts and stops. Then, finally, I got a phone call from your mother saying you were back in Iceland. You had been back for about two weeks and she hadn't bothered to tell me."

I glanced at him, astonished. My mind circled back to that time, to the intense yearning I had to see my father and my grandparents, and how hurt and disappointed I was that they did not come to see us after all the time that had passed. I had asked my mother why, and her response had been vague and unsatisfactory. Now I understood.

"Your mother and I saw each other a few times after you got back …"

"You did?" I was stunned–I'd had no idea. My impression had been that my parents had barely spoken to one another following that sad afternoon when he took me for ice cream and told me that we would no longer be a family.

"We did. We weren't sure what to do; if we should stay married or split up. But it was soon obvious, at least to me, that it wasn't going to work out. Your mother was upset when I started seeing Lísa, she shut me out completely and spoke to me only when absolutely necessary–if it was something to do with you. I was downtown one day, walking up Laugavegur, and when she saw me coming she crossed over to the other side and would not look at me."

"I have this one awful memory of when you came to our house on Christmas Eve with some presents for me," I said.

"Yes," he said, "I remember that. But we had first come the day before, on your birthday–Lísa and I."

I stopped and looked at him. "I don't remember that."

"We had just come from Akureyri and decided to go by the apartment and give you your birthday presents. You were having a party with your friends. Your mother would not let us in to say hello to you, so I came alone the next day, with your birthday and Christmas presents."

The sensation of that visit still felt lodged in my bones–the intense hostility that permeated the air. The following day I had developed an excruciating pain in my belly and was taken to the ER, as it was thought that I might have appendicitis. Yet the doctors could find nothing wrong. It had all been psychosomatic, I realised now–my little child's body unable to hold the searing tension it had absorbed.

"There was also that phone call," I said, thinking out loud.

"What phone call?"

That same evening, Christmas Eve, my father had called after dinner to wish me a Merry Christmas. He, along with the whole family, was at my grandparents' house, and I yearned to be there, too, instead of alone at home with my mother. They passed the phone around so that I could speak to everyone in turn–the next-best thing to being there. We said our goodbyes, but a couple of minutes later the phone rang again. It was my uncle B on the line, saying that someone had not had a chance to talk to me. That someone was Lísa, who had been in the other room. She came on the phone and we talked briefly, wished one another a Merry Christmas, and then hung up. My mother demanded to know to whom I had been speaking. I told her, and watched her countenance grow dark.

"Do you know why she called?" she hissed. The way she said it suggested that *she* knew.

"Because she wanted to wish me a Merry Christmas."

"No," she scoffed. "She didn't want to talk to you. She called to make sure we knew she was there. To make her presence known."

I had not seen what my mother saw–to me, Lísa's call had been without guile.

My father and I walked in silence for a bit. Then, apropos of nothing, he said, "There was this one thing about your mother that always baffled me."

"What?"

"It was when we were starting school at Bifröst. The teacher had this session at the beginning of one of our classes when we had to stand and introduce ourselves–tell the others a bit about who we were. When it came to your mother, she told us that her father worked for the Agricultural Society–that he was a clerk there. Later I found out that her father had died when she was four years old." He paused. "She didn't have a father, but told everyone that she did."

"She lied."

He nodded. "Well ... yes."

"He was an alcoholic, you know," I said.

"I know." He paused, then added. "I think that was one of the things that brought us together. We both had fathers who were alcoholics."

The day before I was to fly back to Toronto, a winter storm blew in–one of those fierce, lashing storms that routinely hits Iceland in the winter and makes us so intensely aware of our own smallness. Yet by evening the world had once more turned calm and benign–the sky twinkled with stars, and a thick layer of pure white snow lay over the ground. I headed outdoors to wade through the snow-filled streets, grateful for the chance to be alone before I packed my suitcase and flew back to my other life. A single band of Aurora swayed overhead, green and luminous and full of grace. I tried to find within myself the girl who had run along these streets with her school bag on her back, or waited at the bus stop for the number five bus to take her into town–to piano lessons, to father's house–but I had left her behind when I assumed my new identity in Canada, and she now eluded me.

Canada. What was it to me now–this place I had called home for the better part of a decade? My mind circled back; memories surfaced. The posse of girls standing at the desk I had chosen on my first day of school; skipping along the street with Piper on a leash; watching The Brady Bunch in Erin and Kevin's rec room; Richard driving me to get my ears pierced and later insisting that I eat my Spam; shivering in the cold basement of the house in Bayridge as I tried to move the rabbit ears on the TV to get reception. Chappy, chained in a corner of the garage. The window in the door. All the ways I had run from what I was feeling: drink, drugs, diets, toxic relationships, frantic exercise, studying, overachieving. Dancing on the edge of an abyss–thinking I had all the answers when I had none.

And finally, Dr. Diamond, who had helped me fumble my way blindfolded through the dark labyrinth in which I was trapped.

I was close to finding the way out. I could feel it.

The following day my father came to take me to the airport, and I hugged my grandmother and grandfather goodbye. As we drove I looked out at the jagged fields of lava that looked so rough and inhospitable from a distance, yet which up close I knew were a wondrous world of spongy moss, hidden crevasses, sheltered hollows and impossibly fragile wildflowers blooming in barren ground in the summers.

I embraced my father, promised to write, then walked stoically into the departures lounge, ready for my transformation from Alda Sigmundsdóttir to Alda Sigmunds.

I gazed through the window as the plane accelerated for take-off, the landscape first blurring and then rushing away as we climbed upward. I saw the air terminal, the US Navy base, the road to Reykjavík with its matchbox-like cars moving along it, and in the distance the capital city, with beautiful, stoic Mt. Esja on the other side of the bay, keeping watch like a sentinel.

The aircraft turned, and we passed through clouds. Iceland

was gone. Ahead lay the relentless beat of the metropolis, my tiny apartment, my stubborn quest for freedom. I leaned the seat back and closed my eyes, fell into a deep repose. Scenes and recollections from the previous two weeks drifted past, as my soul hovered in this liminal space between past and future, gearing itself towards a different place and time. I felt the calm of my grandparents' downstairs apartment, saw the snow on the tree branches in my grandfather's garden in the noonday sun, heard his good-natured guffaw as he threw down his last card after I defeated him in Olsen Olsen–the card game we had always played when I was a child. I thought of the easy stroll with my father along the seaside in Reykjavík, and that thing he had told me just before we parted, about my mother telling everyone she had a father who was a clerk at the Agricultural Society.

My mind slowed, then stopped.

A deliberate lie.

Why?

Probably because she felt insecure and wanted to fit in. It was understandable. I had been desperate to fit in, too, in each of those three schools I'd attended during my first three years in Canada. I even truncated my last name to make it less conspicuous–more "Canadian", whatever that meant. But still, being in her home country and telling a lie that her dead father was still alive when it was so easy for anyone to discover that it was a lie … what had possessed her to do that?

If she lied that she had a father, she must have been tormented about *not* having one. Or tormented by shame about who her father had been–an alcoholic who beat her mother. That knowledge would have only come through hearsay, though, since her father had died when she was only four years old and she would hardly have remembered him. Had her mother told her those things? Had my grandmother talked about my mother's father in the same way my mother had talked to me about my father?

I might never know, but one thing seemed certain: my mother had suffered a deep trauma around the subject of her father, so much that she dared not reveal the truth about him to her classmates. So much that she had to create a fictional father, who was alive, and an upstanding member of society. A fictional father who would put her on par with all the others in her school who had fathers. Because not having a father made her *less-than.* Because not having a father made her ashamed.

She had never spoken to me about any of this. She had barely spoken of her father at all, in fact. I tried to conjure up the few details I knew about him: he had been an alcoholic and had been violent while drunk–I had learned this from Klara, who told me she had once seen him coming down the stairs with a knife in his hand, threatening to kill her mother; he'd had an aptitude for drawing, as evidenced by a charcoal picture that hung on our living room wall when I was a child; he had died of consumption, an illness exacerbated by his alcoholism.

That was about it.

Now there was evidence that my mother's father had left a deep laceration on her soul, even though she had never known him. This pain and trauma of hers had never been visible to me.

Or had it?

Wounds to the soul, when left untreated, do not simply vanish. This much I had learned through my sessions with Dr. Diamond. They always manifest in some way in the life of the person carrying the wound. I had also learned that if a woman is wounded by her father and she has not done the work required to heal, that wound will almost always manifest in her relationships with men.

So there was my mother telling a lie about her father at the same time as she was about to embark on a relationship with the man who would become her husband and the father of her child–*my* father.

There is a force in every human being that always and

unfailingly strives towards wholeness. When we are physically wounded, whether it is a cut to our finger or a broken bone, our body immediately rallies to try to heal us. Even when the body is unable to fix something on its own–say a broken bone that needs to be set by a doctor if it is to heal properly–it nevertheless tries its best. And if we want to live, we must surrender to the force that makes us whole–that is our only choice.

Psychic wounds are not different from physical wounds–the only difference is that they are not visible to the eye. If we receive a serious physical injury, most of us will immediately go to a hospital. If we experience a serious psychic injury, we are far less likely to seek help. Perhaps because we want to deny the trauma, or cannot understand it, or are ashamed of what happened to us, or do not have the resources to cope. Or perhaps we have been taught to keep the psychic injury secret, because revealing it would shed light on something shameful or taboo. Or we are convinced that we deserved the wound, because we brought it on ourselves, or are in some way deficient.

In the same way our body tries to heal itself, our psyches want to move us towards wholeness. Yet our unconscious goes about this in a somewhat misguided way: it draws us to or recreates circumstances similar to the original hurt, hoping to "fix" the trauma.

"Imagine that you are a film projector," Dr. Diamond had said when I was terrified of random people on the street and their judgmental gaze. "The film is inside of you, but as you move through life you project your film onto other people. What you are seeing is not objective reality, but the film playing inside your own self."

Inside herself, my mother held an image of what she believed would save her from her trauma, and she projected that image onto my father. She needed him to be the perfect bridegroom-slash-father, who loved and took care of her. She moreover needed him to be the ideal lover and husband, the provider of an ideal marriage that would be superimposed onto the broken world from which she came, and protect her from the shame and hurt inside of her own self.

Of itself, this is not unusual. Many people form illusions to help them cope with trauma and pain. I did it, too–I believed that my family in Iceland, and especially my father, would be able to save me from my inner damage. That did not happen, of course; instead I fell into a black hole. This, in turn, led me to Dr. Diamond, and the process of trying to excavate a truth that would help me grow a life. That, I know now, is the healthy response when one's fantasies do not work out–we examine our lives and expectations, and make the adjustments required to build a better future. Very often this involves finding a level of humility–realising that life, and other people, do not owe us anything. It also means absorbing the knowledge that we cannot superimpose our wills onto other people and make them conform to an image that we have created inside our heads. It doesn't work that way–and moreover, it is wrong. Others should be free to live their lives according to their own destinies. To live out God's–or, if you prefer, Life's–plan.

When my father failed to live up to my mother's expectations, when he turned out to be just a flawed, imperfect child of an alcoholic like her, she had two choices: honest self-reflection and an acceptance of her pain, or the casting of herself as victim, with my father as perpetrator. If you have read this far in my story, you will know which she chose. I do not say that to cast blame–if she'd had the resources to do things differently, she likely would have. There but for the grace of God … and all that.

The collapse of my mother's marriage to my father represented not only the collapse of their relationship, but also of her fragile identity. And so, in a feeble attempt to remain intact, she ran away to a different country. For two years she avoided facing the inevitable truth: that my father could not provide her with the glue that she believed would hold her together.

These revelations unfolded behind my closed eyelids as I sat in a deep, almost hypnotic, reverie. One by one they revealed themselves, stacking up into a new vision of the world, and of my life. It felt to me that I had always known the things that were so gently and delicately being held up for me to see, just as I had forever possessed the knowledge of things that Sam and I had talked about inside our little circle of light down in that dingy Cabbagetown bar.

I suddenly began thinking about a film I had seen a month or so earlier. There was an Ingmar Bergman retrospective on at the Art Gallery of Ontario and I had bought a pass, having become infatuated with Bergman's work after watching his film *Fanny and Alexander.* The first movie I saw in the retrospective was called *Persona*–one of Bergman's early works. In it, two women have retreated to an isolated island together–an actress who has inexplicably stopped talking, and a psychiatric nurse who has been hired to take care of her. As the actress sits in stoic silence, she becomes a blank canvas onto which the nurse can project her expectations and needs. She begins to tell the actress intimate details of her life, eventually spilling one of her deepest secrets. In that solitude, a strange, symbiotic relationship forms, as if the two women have merged psychologically, effectively becoming one person in two bodies. Bergman is very explicit about his meaning, actually merging the faces of the two women–a cinematic novelty at the time. Eventually the nurse discovers that the actress has been studying, observing and forming her own judgements of her behind her impassive exterior. The nurse becomes enraged. The image she projected onto the actress was her own construct, yet instead of seeing where she, herself, was at fault, she turns her hatred towards the person who has failed to carry her projection for her.

I left the theatre that day, a dirty, grey December day, oddly preoccupied with the film. It was as if something niggled at me, something I needed to know–a message that was being conveyed, but which I was as yet unable to grasp.

Now, with this memory unfolding, I had a flash of insight: *That is what happened between my mother and me.*

A psychological merging.

I recalled, then, a dream I'd had about a year after I started seeing Dr. Diamond. In it I was wandering the corridors of the hospital where Dr. Diamond worked, desperate to find him, for I urgently needed to tell him something. Then, suddenly, my mother stood in the centre of the corridor, towering over me. Over to the side stood Klara. Taking hold of my shoulder, my mother ushered me into a bright, white, windowless room and closed the door. I quivered–I knew she was angry. Looming above me, she demanded to know what it was that I was planning to tell Dr. Diamond. I was silent and stared at the floor, for what I had to say was precious and fragile, and for his ears only. I could sense my mother's fury, and knew she would not release me from the room unless I told her what I wanted to tell him. I was trapped, entirely in her power. And so, I told her. As I surrendered the precious thing I had held so carefully, I felt a torrent of shame, because in so doing I knew I had not only betrayed Dr. Diamond, but also the most pure and truthful part of myself. My mother appeared satisfied, and opened the door for me to exit. As we emerged Klara turned to look at me, and I felt a crushing shame, as though I had been grossly violated.

Dr. Diamond had listened to me relate the dream, then asked gently, "What was it you wanted to tell me?"

"I don't know."

He waited a moment, then said: "I think it's obvious, don't you?"

I shook my head. "No."

"Well, it seems to me that in the dream I represented your father, and you wanted to tell me that you loved me. But your mother insisted that you tell her–that you give *her* your love, instead."

In the vision of my life that was now appearing, that dream made perfect sense. Rather than allowing me to have my feelings for my father, she had demanded I turn them over to her. She had wanted me to feel about my father exactly like she had felt about her father. A dark wound bled within her, and she could not abide watching her own daughter have a relationship with a loving father when she, herself, had wanted exactly that.

It now struck me, hard: In order to escape her pain, and for her to continue to function in the world, my mother needed me to be exactly like her. "It was like she got more and more resentful of us, like she thought we were having too much of an influence over you," my grandmother had said. She was right. My mother *had* been losing me to them because I sought all ways to escape from that metaphorical white room–which at that time was the apartment I lived in with my mother. I had clung to my grandparents to escape my mother's insistence on solidarity, her demand that I should merge with her in that dark place; to become one soul in two bodies, like the two women in *Persona.*

Was this even possible?

Was it really possible for two people to merge like that? For one person to surrender her entire being to another? All her thoughts, convictions, beliefs, identity, *selfhood*? And was that what had happened to me ... had I effectively *disappeared* into my mother?

She had never truly acknowledged my separateness from her. I saw that now. Everything I said or did she took personally, or perceived as a personal indignity. When as a young girl I was at my aunt and uncle's place, so unhappy I wanted to die, she had declared me "selfish" and "thinking only of yourself" when I asked for her protection. My feelings had been inconvenient to her, so she had shamed me. I was a liability, not a frightened child who needed her mother. When I had been given the impossible task of babysitting an older cousin who wound up having an agenda of her own, I was a "disgrace" to our family. And on numerous occasions over the years, she had chided me for having been so "cruel" to her when I was a child. When I finally asked her how, exactly, that cruelty had manifested, she said that I'd come home and asked her why we could not have nice furniture like a friend in my class, when I should have known she could not afford it.

And I had believed her. I had internalised it all.

Yet on some deep level I could not accept the obliteration of my own identity, and the way she had desecrated the tender feelings I had for my father's side of the family. I held my feelings in, terrified to incur her wrath, until they gushed forth like water from a broken fire hydrant. Oh how terrified I had been to speak out with my own voice–so terrified that I had felt the need to barricade myself in the bathroom.

It had been a bold move, opening my mouth to shout my truth, and it had been possible only–*only*–because there were people near me that had my back. I was confident that, if my mother were to cast me aside, my grandparents would take me in. Then my mother took me to see a psychiatrist because we were "fighting so much"– now I saw that fight for what it was: a battle to retain my own soul. The doctor had told my mother that I was normal, and that she should bring me to see him only when we *stopped* fighting. He had recognised the danger of my submission.

We had stopped fighting. We *had* stopped fighting when my mother insisted I go with her to Canada. There I could no longer afford the luxury of rebellion because I needed her too much. With no options left, I surrendered. I became numb and ceased to be guided by my own internal compass. I cleaved, instead, to my mother. Much, perhaps, as she cleaved to Richard–he of the uniforms, the swords, the cannon holsters, the master's chair, the party line. He who believed that dogs should be disciplined and kept chained in the corner of the garage for 23 hours a day. Who obsessed over the length of my showers, the setting of the thermostat, and every other minute detail of the household.

The little girl–my mother–who had no father, who was too

ashamed to reveal the truth about her daddy to the world, had found the strong man she had longed for to heal her wound.

But oh, little girl. Such a wound is not healed in that way.

No one has the power to illuminate your darkness but you.

She stayed, despite Richard's manipulations and tyranny. She kept up appearances: accompanying her soldier to the dinners and balls, erecting a white picket fence around their idyllic homestead, so that no one could see through to the meanness beneath.

How did she do it? I wondered silently to myself. *How could she bear to live with that man?*

The answer came, from that same deep place that was offering up these delicate revelations, one by one: *her relationship with Richard was conditional on you carrying her darkness–her rage, hate, hurt, trauma–*for *her. As long as she could project it onto* you, *see it in* you, *she could ignore it in herself, and carry on.*

Those two women merging in Bergman's film.

My mother's relationship with Richard had been conditional on our "sisterhood", on me merging with her in that dark place and hating him, so that she could be free to love him.

Was this … even possible?

My rational mind wavered, doubted–but deep inside I felt *a knowing.*

A dysfunctional union always seeks to isolate and to hide. My mother and Richard decided to move to the countryside, into even more isolation than before. My mother's assumption was that I would accompany her, as I had always done. Yet by then I instinctively knew that my spirit would not survive it. At the same time my greatest, most suffocating, fear was manifesting: my mother was abandoning me. It was the dread that had underpinned my entire life, that kept me obedient and deferential. It seemed to me that we had made a silent pact. The pact was that if I gave up my life, my self, my opinions, my beliefs, my home and the people I loved, she would stay with me and protect me.

Yet she did not.

Instead, I got my own little temple, where at seventeen I was thrust into the role of landlord, manager and adult. The persona I had assumed–a carbon copy of my mother–remained loyal to her, and disloyal to myself. Inside a part of me screamed for recognition of the truth: the betrayal, the fear, the loss of identity.

Shane had merely been incidental to the implosion of my self, as Dr. Diamond had observed when I sat in his office on that first day and blithely informed him that I was all better now because my bad feelings had been carried off by someone I had rejected.

The malignancy had been much, much deeper and more complex: he saw that instantly.

And so, we had set about the surgery.

Caught up as I was in treading water, I failed to notice that a crack had begun to form in my relations with my mother. The signs were so subtle that perhaps it was not strange that they should go undetected. Now, putting that time under the magnifying glass, I saw there had been a strange sort of indifference in my mother's attitude to everything I was doing. Even more: there was an aversion, almost a fear. Looking down on my life now from a vantage point of 30,000 feet, it was suddenly obvious to me that my mother had been very threatened when I started opening up the old stuffy trunks in the attic that was our joint past. Like the nurse in Bergman's film, the blank canvas onto which she had projected her own image suddenly began to have thoughts, feelings, opinions and insights of her own. This angered her. That was why she had diminished my struggle, minimised my anguish, dismissed my pain. She had not come to visit me in Toronto because to do so would force her to admit that I had a life separate from hers–that she and I were *not* one person, that I had *not* been created to carry her shadow for her, but was in fact a person struggling to reclaim my own identity. She knew she was losing her hold over me–that soon she would not be able to rely on me as a psychological crutch. When I burned that role to the ground she would be left with all the terrible things inside her from which she had spent her life trying to run–all the things that had been projected onto me, and which I had carried.

And so, she had decided to have another baby.

Was I crazy?

After all, there was nothing unusual about a woman wanting to have a baby with her husband.

Yet my mother and Richard had been together for eight years without trying for a baby, and now–as soon as I was breaking free–she suddenly decided that she wanted another. Before that time, I had never once heard my mother say that she wanted another child. I remembered when I told her that I was seeing Manuel, and she snapped, "Don't expect me to raise your child for you if you get pregnant!" And then, that bizarre remark when she told me of her own pregnancy: "Since there was little chance you would have one for me, I figured I would have to do it myself."

The remark had been so odd, so absurd. Yet now I wondered: could it be that she had viewed us as effectively one and the same person, and that if I had a child, it would be her child, too?

Or did she choose to have another baby because she needed a replacement? Was it my sister Frannie's destiny to carry my mother's darkness, in lieu of me? I was the disloyal daughter who had betrayed my mother–that, I recognised now, had been her message to me when I last saw her. Her cold aloofness, her focus on my sister, her silent fury at me. *You are dismissed.* You are no longer needed here. You have chosen *them* over *me*, and therefore you are nothing to me.

Was I losing my mind?

What I needed now, more than anything, was a trustworthy person to listen and tell me if I was eminently lucid, or stark raving mad. Like Sue Ellen in Dallas, I needed my therapist.

❦

I had an appointment with Dr. Diamond three days after my return. Never had I felt a greater urgency to see him. The extraordinary lucidity I'd had on the airplane turned murky as old dish water the moment I stepped off the plane and felt familiar surroundings close around me. Three days felt more like three months. When I at last sat in the padded armchair in Dr. Diamond's consulting room, I wondered if I had the words to articulate what I needed to say. Thoughts and images flashing through my mind was one thing; formulating them into coherent sentences was quite another.

"You had a good trip?" he said, his manner breezy.

I nodded, and after giving him a brief rundown of my visit to Iceland, took a deep breath. "There is something my father told me that has given me a lot to think about and I don't know if I'm crazy."

Sensing my gravity, his face grew serious and he settled into his chair. "Okay. Let's hear it."

"It's … it has to do with my mother. I don't really know where to begin."

"Begin anywhere."

It came out in bits, and in no particular order. My mother's lie to her classmates. The deep trauma, inadequacy and shame it implied. The hypothesis I constructed in my airplane seat: how she had worked to eliminate my father from our lives because my relationship with him reminded her too much of her own pain. How she demanded my allegiance and how that was the subtext of all our interactions. Her standoffishness towards me at Klara's place before I left. The anger that erupted in me on the drive back to Toronto. The phone call to my mother the following day; my longing for her call afterwards, that never came. My grandmother's speculation about my mother taking me to Canada to escape my grandparents' influence. The thing my father had told me about coming to my birthday party and being refused entry. How I had surrendered my self to my mother when we moved to Canada because I was terrified she would leave me, and if that happened I would be in mortal danger. How I had unwittingly agreed to carry her darkness. The way we had, effectively, merged. Whether it could be that my inability to have intimate relationships was really *her* inability to have intimate relationships. How on some deep unspoken level I had carried her anger and distrust of Richard *for* her. How, when I refused to move with her to the farm, she had begun to grow distant, and how that chasm had grown wider when I left for Toronto and began to examine pieces of the past. How she might have been subtly punishing me, for instance by not coming to see me or caring about my predicament. How she needed to see me as an extension of herself, and whether that, too, was why she had never come–because she would then have to acknowledge my separateness, and take responsibility for her own darkness. Whether my sister was my replacement–whether my mother had decided, at that specific point in time, to have another child because I had left her, both literally and psychically, and she needed a psychological crutch. Whether the reason for my perpetual shame was that I had yearned to have my needs met, but had learned that I was bad and wrong to want this because the only needs that mattered were my mother's. Whether my self-hatred might be my mother's internalised rage towards me for daring to be a separate person from her.

As I spoke I glanced at Dr. Diamond repeatedly to check whether he was following this disjointed narrative, hyper-alert for signs of disapproval or mockery. I kept expecting to see him suppress a laugh or try to hide his scorn, but he did neither. Instead, he seemed captivated by what I was saying. When I finally slowed, and then stopped, he gave a tiny shake of his head. My heart dropped like a stone. He didn't believe me. My ideas were the fabrications of a sick mind.

But to my astonishment, he said, "So it was your mother all along."

It took me a moment. I blinked. Then I blurted out: "So you are saying this makes sense?"

He nodded, his face grim. "It makes perfect sense."

CHAPTER 26

I DON'T KNOW, EXACTLY, when the conviction came to me that I must leave Canada. Perhaps I already knew on that plane, when the truth appeared, tranquil and sweet, like a whisper. Or when I found myself again on the streets of Toronto and realised that while everything was familiar, nothing was familiar. It was as though I had awoken from a deep sleep to find myself wandering through a foreign land, without entirely knowing how I got there.

Numerous times over the previous two years I had wanted to run, to bolt. To go live somewhere else, find a life … somewhere else. But where? I was never quite sure. And Dr. Diamond had dissuaded me, pointing out that I would be the same person in that other place; just as lost, just as scared. "When you have found yourself," he said, "you can go anywhere."

Had I found myself now? Was it safe for me to go? I did not know; did not trust this new person I had found within, who still needed so much nurturing and coaxing to grow into her own character, and identity, and feelings.

"I think it is a good idea," Dr. Diamond said when I anxiously broached the subject, his eyes twinkling with subdued affection and something that looked like fatherly pride. "Iceland is your home. You have people there who care for you, and will support you. That is what you need now. Go."

I exhaled. I had wished for his blessing, and he had given it.

Things needed to be wrapped up. I had to withdraw from university, put my house in Kingston on the market, sell my car, pack up the few belongings I planned to take with me.

And I needed to confront my mother.

I had to prove to myself that I could withstand her projections, and the self-erasure I felt in her presence. I had to prove that I could stand before her and speak my truth. "She's not that powerful," Dr. Diamond had said when I talked to him about my fear that the sheer force of her presence might obliterate this tiny budding self that was pushing up out of the rubble. But I knew he was wrong: she *was* that powerful. She had created me in her own image and so, I felt, she had the power to annihilate me.

It was a cold, bright day in January, the day I set out for my mother and Richard's farm. The farther away from Toronto I drove, the more my convictions slipped away. Mental paralysis overtook me, erasing my truth, eroding my thoughts, filling me with doubts. I saw myself standing small and powerless before my mother, compelled to say things I did not want to say, speaking words I had not meant to speak. Not in possession of myself, but possessed by something else. I considered stopping the car and turning back, or bypassing the farm and going straight through to Kingston. But I knew I could not. If I was ever to be free, this was something I had to do.

At last her house came into view–white clapboard with black

shutters, set in a white landscape, with one spindly tree next to it. Heart thumping, I turned off the main road and up my mother's driveway. There was just the whisper of a breeze; apart from that, all was silent. I stepped out of the car, made my way to the front door, knocked. It opened, and I stood facing my mother. She looked as if she had been expecting me. I noticed her eyes, and suddenly recognised a look in them that I had seen many times: deep, buried rage–the kind that does not want to be disturbed.

We stared at one another for a moment, not speaking. Then one side of her mouth curved upwards, and she stepped aside to let me in.

We stood there in the middle of the kitchen, staring at one another.

"I've decided to move back to Iceland," I began.

She looked at me, that supercilious smirk still there. "Did you come here to tell me that?"

My heart began to race. "No," I said. "Not only that."

"Oh?" she said, crossing her arms. "What else?"

My breath grew shallow and I had a sudden sense that all the air was being sucked out of the room.

"You brought me to Canada," I said. "I didn't want to come here. I wanted to stay with my father."

She remained still, staring at me, still smirking. "Yes. You always idolised him," she said calmly.

I felt a surge of anger. "He loved me," I said hotly. "He said I could go and stay …"

She cut me off, the smirk gone now. "Why didn't you go? Eh? You had the chance to go. You knew that after a year you were free to leave. Why didn't you?"

I faltered. I couldn't formulate in my mind what I knew–that there was no way that, at age eleven, I could have made a choice to leave my primary caregiver, with whom I had moreover formed a trauma bond.

"You're accusing *me* of keeping you here, but the truth was that *you* didn't want to leave. *You* didn't want to live with your father."

"I did *not* want to leave Iceland. You made me come with you, and when you had no use for me anymore, you just dumped me!" My voice was becoming shrill.

She gave a short, sharp laugh. "Dumped you!? Hardly. What did you expect … that I would choose *you* over Richard?"

"… You needed me to come here with you because you needed me to be just like you. You didn't want me to have a relationship with my father because *you* didn't have a father!"

For a moment her jaw slackened, then she narrowed her eyes. "Who the hell do you think you are, coming here and accusing me …."

"Why did you take me from the people who loved me? And then just *drop* me?"

"Your grandparents you mean? They gave you *money*. That was the extent of their 'love'." She spat the last word, as though it was abhorrent to her.

Words tumbled out of me, rapid and incoherent. "You needed me to be a mirror of you. You couldn't go on unless you had me carry your *shit* for you. You have no idea who you are. You think you're such a good mother? You promised me I could have a dog if I came with you … and then you get Richard a dog!"

Her face flushed with anger. "I know you would not have looked after a dog at that age! It would have been up to *me* to take care of it."

"You know what? You can't see your own fault in anything. You can't take any responsibility for anything."

"Oh, I see plenty. You know what I see? A stupid 21-year-old who thinks she has all the answers. Someone who comes here to attack me–after everything you've been given. Poor little rich girl. But I'm not surprised. You were always cruel to me. You were a cruel, spiteful child, even when we lived in Iceland. Yes–I regret what I did. I regret bringing you with me. I should have left you with your father."

"I wish you had!"

She snorted, then took a step closer to me and looked into my face, her mouth tight with anger, or disgust, or both. When she spoke, her voice was low and deliberate. "I see you for what you are. You're a *snake.* You *live* to hurt people."

I opened my mouth to say something, but nothing came out. Something about her words and demeanour chilled me to the marrow, and I knew that I would have to leave, to go, *immediately.*

I have no idea how long I stayed. I do not remember how I left, or if my mother and I exchanged words when I did. I suspect that my description of events is not perfectly accurate, but I do know that all of those words–the ones I wrote above–were spoken during our confrontation.

When I set out for my mother's farm that day I might have harboured a vague hope that we could talk things through. That she might try to see my point of view. See *me*, even, and herself–at least in part. That we might be able to settle our differences, and move towards a real, loving, relationship.

I had no idea of what I was up against.

Confronting someone like my mother is like confronting a demonic force. Speaking truth to them is like throwing holy water on a demon. It will hiss and spit and writhe and lunge and seek to destroy.

In his book *People of the Lie–the Hope for Healing Human Evil*, psychiatrist M. Scott Peck, now deceased, writes about narcissism and the concept of evil. In one of the chapters he describes an exchange with his eight-year-old son, who remarks to his father, "Why, Daddy, 'evil' is 'live' spelled backward."

This beautifully lucid observation perfectly encapsulates what it is to have suffered abuse from a narcissist, or someone with a severe personality disorder. The toxic force that possesses them and gradually enmeshes their victims is *evil*–the opposite of "live". People who objectify and dehumanise others and force them to carry their darkness, they do not give life. They *take* life.

When I tried to get my life back, I was constantly pulled down by the force that wanted to keep me from being alive–that wanted to keep me in darkness. I was possessed by evil.

I know: evil is a loaded word, one we have come to associate with horrific crimes–the Holocaust, slavery, genocide, torture, murder. Yet evil is not something distant or abstract. Whenever one person insists on imposing their will on another, there is evil. Whenever someone sees others merely as vehicles for their own advancement or stimulation, there is evil. Whenever there is energy that tears down instead of builds up, there is evil. Whenever cold calculation replaces love and empathy, there is evil.

Evil is all around us. It is commonplace. It exists not only in the darkest pockets of society, but also behind the pretty facades of perfect homes with picket fences. And those who commit evil are often perfectly nice folks whose right hand is completely unaware of what their left hand is doing. They do not see their actions as reprehensible. They see them as rational.

Evil kills–sometimes physically; always spiritually. It kills enthusiasm, love, joy, spontaneity, laughter. It kills dreams and potential. And sometimes it causes people to kill themselves.

CHAPTER 27

WHEN I LEFT MY mother's house on the day of our reckoning I drove to Kingston, put my house on the market, then headed back to Toronto to begin dismantling my life.

Three months later, I was in Iceland, staying with my father and Vera. Their renovation was complete, and they were back in their own home where they had invited me to stay while I looked for my own apartment. Our relations were still brittle, but we had a tacit agreement that we wanted to make things work.

I relished being back among my tribe–that sense of belonging. There was quiet joy in the simple things, like no longer having to spell my name for anyone who needed to write it down, or explain that the reason Sigmundsdóttir sounded like "Sigmund's daughter" was because that is precisely what it was.

Iceland was my motherland. I was Iceland's daughter.

My maternal grandmother, Ella, turned 80 that spring, and a celebration was planned at the home of my aunt Alma, whose daughter, Hrefna, I had lost all those years ago. It was to be what the Icelanders call *ættarmót*–a gathering of the extended family. I was invited, and through some subtle questioning I managed to glean that my mother would not be attending. That was not a surprise–she was a busy woman, as I well knew. Besides, she had renounced–and denounced–Iceland years earlier, and had only visited once in the decade since she had moved to Canada. I was extremely relieved that she would not be there. The memory of our last encounter still stung, and the mere thought of seeing her caused my anxiety to soar.

Klara, however, was planning to come, and I was glad. Though I knew that she would always be in my mother's corner, I felt we had a bond. Three days before the party I was at my father and Vera's, helping to clear up after dinner. The phone rang and my father answered, then passed it to me. It was Klara. She said hello, asked how I was doing, and we made casual conversation. Her voice sounded upbeat and just a tiny bit strained. As we talked I began to feel an undercurrent to our exchange–a sense that there was something she was not saying. Indeed, it was a tad perplexing that she should call me at all–we were not in the habit of speaking on the phone unless there was something specific to arrange. Finally, after a round of small talk, she mentioned, in a by-the-by sort of way, that my mother was with her, and would be at the party.

I felt a *whoosh* of black fear, and in an instant I knew: my mother had come to stake her claim. This was her last-ditch effort to assert her ownership over me.

I put down the phone and stared straight ahead, my primal instincts on red alert. The strength I had managed to accumulate over the past few weeks would be annihilated in my mother's presence. The toxic cloud would swallow me and I would wind up feeling contaminated, ugly, hateful, *a disgrace to the family.* There would be self-loathing, and that awful feeling of not being myself, but my mother. I couldn't do it. I would have to cancel, find some excuse for why I couldn't go to my grandmother's party.

She's not that powerful.

Dr. Diamond's words. There were people in this world like him, like Sam, like many, many others–people who supported me and wanted me to thrive. Even if mother, that powerful, omniscient archetype, had failed to nurture and protect; even if my own *mother* considered me *selfish* and *a snake*, it did not mean that the entire world did.

I had not done anything wrong. I had merely claimed my right to my own life.

I would go.

Standing in front of Alma's large, functional-style house I could hear the buzz of voices coming from inside, up on the second floor. The party was underway.

The day before I had spoken to one of my cousins, who in a roundabout way had told me that my mother had not wanted me to know she was coming. I knew why. She planned to catch me off guard. She was preparing an ambush.

The front door stood open. Taking a deep breath, I stepped inside. In front of me was the wide, Scandi-minimalist staircase that led to the main floor. I ascended slowly. When I got to the top of the stairs I paused–to the right of me was a small alcove and through there the main entrance to the party; to the left was the kitchen. If I passed through there I would enter the party through the dining area, which would make me less conspicuous than if I went through the main doorway.

I turned left.

In the kitchen were Alma, Hrefna, and two other women I did not know; I greeted them, we exchanged a few words, and I threaded my way past them, to the main room.

The large dining table was laden with hors d'oeuvres, open-faced sandwiches, crudités. A few people milled about, looking ready to pounce on the refreshments once the host said *Gjörið svo vel*–"please begin". I turned, nearly colliding with an elderly gentleman whom I could not remember meeting before.

"Hello!" he said cheerfully, his watery blue eyes twinkling, "whose daughter are you?"

In Icelandic that question can mean two things: *Whose daughter are you?* and *What is your last name?*

I ascribed that second meaning to his question, and was about to tell him, but before I could speak I heard a loud voice ring out, cutting through the party hum.

"Hún er Elísabetardóttir."

She is Elísabet's daughter.

The room quieted. Heads turned to look at my mother and then at me.

There it was.

She sat in a far corner. I saw her eyes. They had that deep, enraged look I had observed when she opened the door to me at the farm, the last time we had met.

"She is *my* daughter," she said decisively.

I stared back and felt a strange, unexpected calm come over me, as though something had moved in, silent and stealthy, and was weaving itself around me–a tender, ironclad caul of safety and protection.

She's not that powerful.

I turned back to the kindly man with the blue eyes who stood there waiting for an answer–not from my mother, but from *me.*

Extending my hand, I said: "My name is Alda Sigmundsdóttir."

EPILOGUE

Naturally, my story does not end there. The conditioning of a lifetime is not undone with a single act of rebellion, no matter how momentous it may seem at the time.

I fell back into numbness and complacency; doubted my memories, my perception and even my sanity. "It wasn't all that bad," droned my subconscious, "you over-dramatised it, made a big deal out of nothing".

Mostly, though, I just ceased to remember, and got on with life as best I could.

My mother and I went through a period of no contact, and also of minimal contact. When I found myself pregnant and alone and living in a foreign country I foolishly allowed myself to trust her again, and to reach for the helping hand she extended. Alas, the hand was swiftly withdrawn and I was subjected to her scathing vituperation once more. After that incident, which was particularly egregious, I vowed I would never ask her for anything on my own behalf again. I kept that promise.

Though I went back to Iceland in the winter of 1984 with the intention of making my life there, it would nevertheless be a decade before I fully settled in my native country. In the interim I drifted–moving first back to Canada, then to England, then Spain, and finally to Germany. I returned to Iceland in 1994, then with a three-year-old daughter of my own.

My mother visited Iceland from time to time, and my daughter Aldís and I usually saw her during those visits, at least once. Soon she began broaching the subject of Aldís coming to Canada to stay with her at the farm–something that, as far as I was concerned, was entirely out of the question.

The topic was revived one night when, at the end of one of her visits, I was saying goodbye to her on the stoop of her sister's house. She had been drinking, and there had been a tense situation a few minutes earlier, when she began picking at a metaphorical scab, trying to create drama. By now I recognised this trick, and had learned not to engage. Instead I had calmly risen and announced that it was time for me and Aldís to leave.

As she embraced my daughter, she cooed, "Maybe soon mamma will let you come visit me and all the animals!"

My stomach clenched as I ushered Aldís into the back seat of my car and fastened her seatbelt.

My mother dropped her tone. "It's all right for you to send her, you know. The power has shifted."

Straightening up, I turned to her. "What do you mean?"

The corner of her mouth curved upward. "I have the power now."

I shook my head, not comprehending.

"Richard has a secret," she added, pausing for effect.

I shook my head again with slight irritation. I was weary of her games.

The story came out in increments over the next two weeks. Via email she told me that, for years, Richard had engaged in compulsive behaviour of which he was deeply ashamed. He was able to keep it hidden while he still left the farm each day for work, but after he retired it became harder to conceal. One day, by chance, my mother found out.

This secret of Richard's was not one that caused harm to anyone, except perhaps Richard himself and those who sustained collateral damage as a result of his relentless self-flagellation. Suddenly Richard's crazy behaviour throughout the years, his obsessive need to control and shame others, began to make sense.

The strong man that my mother had hoped would heal her psychic wound had turned out to be a flawed, imperfect human, just like my own father had, all those years before.

Narcissistic relationships are about power. Since a narcissist cannot feel empathy, real love or deep connection is absent. Narcissists become addicted to power over another in the same way an addict craves a fix. This "drug" that the narcissist craves is known as narcissistic supply.

For years, my mother derived her narcissistic supply from me. When I was no longer there to provide it, I was dismissed, and replaced. When my father betrayed my mother's expectations of him, she withdrew access to herself, and to me, as a form of punishment.

Now it was Richard's turn.

Again, my mother withdrew access to herself and her daughter. Only, this time she did not leave. Instead, she built an actual wall through the house she shared with Richard, dividing "his" side from "hers". She installed a bathroom and a kitchen, and retreated into her adopted bunker with Frances. From inside it my mother could wield Richard's weakness like a weapon against him, vilifying him for his depravity and casting herself in the role of martyr. It was the perfect setup, for martyrs are always absolved of blame. Richard carried the burden of her darkness, and my mother was whitewashed, as before.

How ironic that, in the end, it should be Richard who carried my mother's projections; her shame. And through it all, Frances came to hate her father so much that she was ready to slash her wrists if it meant getting rid of his DNA from her body, as she announced in my kitchen that day when she visited me in Reykjavík.

In August 2006, my mother went into the hospital for a procedure to remove tumours from her lower abdomen that were thought to be benign. They were not. My mother had cancer.

The shock of the diagnosis seemed to penetrate her emotional barrier in a way that nothing had before. She began to examine her life and to make significant changes–switching to a new and healthier diet, paying attention to how her lifestyle might affect her health, and even seeing a psychologist–a major breakthrough, for she had always considered other people to be root of all her problems. She also began to think seriously about ending her marriage to Richard.

In February 2007, she suddenly fell ill and was rushed to hospital. An examination showed that a rapid, cancerous growth had blocked her bowel. Two days later, she died.

I was at home in Iceland when I got the news. Right away I began making arrangements to travel to Canada. It never occurred to me not to go. Yet speaking to Klara on the phone the following evening, I noticed a strange reticence on her end of the line. My mother had asked to be cremated and not embalmed, she told me, and the funeral would be in four days' time. That was hardly enough time for me to get there. Besides, it was expensive for me to fly over at such short notice. Would it not be better for me to wait until she, Jim, Billy, Sara and Frances brought my mother's ashes to Iceland in early summer? We would then have a memorial service for her there–perhaps I could arrange that?

In the midst of my emotional turmoil, her dissuasion hit me

hard. Clearly I was not wanted there. The old pain rushed forth and I felt utterly debilitated.

A few days later I understood the real reason behind Klara's discouragement. She knew that flights were costly, and also that I was to receive no inheritance from my mother. I was not even mentioned in her will. Frances was the sole beneficiary of my mother's estate, which comprised her half of the farm, and money in various bank accounts. I had already received my inheritance, Klara said–the apartment my parents had put into my name all those years earlier, so my mother and I would always have a place to live. The same apartment that later facilitated her abandonment of me.

Even in death, my mother was able to deal one final, dismissive blow.

A few months after my mother's death, Richard began seeing a woman he had known for a number of years, and moved in with her. He also took to sending me Christmas cards. Stunned as I was by this, it was nothing next to the shock I felt at receiving a letter from him in which he asked me to forgive him for the way he had treated me as a child.

It was an apology I readily accepted.

Richard died in 2015, of heart failure.

All those years ago in Toronto, when I went out walking at night, I would look in through illuminated windows at what I imagined to be happy and serene families in their lovely and beautiful homes. The simple pleasures they enjoyed–flopping on the sofa watching a film with a loved one; cooking dinner with friends–I felt convinced would never be mine. I would forever be an outsider looking in, trapped in my private darkness. To live, *really* live, amongst people–that was reserved for others, not for me.

Today, four decades later, I live a life of grace. All the things I dreamed of, that I believed would never be mine–a caring family, a loving partner, emotional stability, a thriving career, even a wonderful dog … all of this and more has manifested in my life.

I thought I was irreparably broken, but I discovered that it is possible to be whole again.

To be loved.

To be at peace.

To be enough.

Before I close ...

If you feel unseen, I see you.
If you were abused, I see you.
If you were neglected or shunned, I see you.
If you were abandoned, I see you.
If you carry guilt or shame, I see you.
If you feel worthless, I see you.
If you fear annihilation, I see you.
If you battle the darkness, I see you.

You are beautiful.
You are worthy.
You are needed.
You are not alone.

ACKNOWLEDGEMENTS

First of all, I would like to acknowledge the fact that this book was enormously hard to write. Even though decades have passed since these events occurred, the moment I opened the compartment in my soul where they resided, the old fear and dread came rushing back. Along with this came the voice that incessantly whispered that I had it all wrong, that I was over-dramatizing, that it didn't really happen that way. Once more I doubted my perception of reality.

Yet over the years I have grown more adept at handling this unwelcome intruder. Whereas in the beginning I showed up to the battle with nothing more than the metaphoric equivalent of a loincloth, I am now clad in full armour, and have learned to wield a sword.

Part of that is knowing when and where to ask for help. To the two women who came to my aid during this process, SP and EJ–thank you for believing my story, and for mirroring back the reality of who I am.

My gratitude goes out to my daughter Aldís Amah, for teaching me so much and working with me to break the generational cycle; my husband Erlingur Páll, for listening to and supporting me even when he didn't fully understand; and to everyone along the way–in Canada, Germany and Iceland–who has helped me to heal.

Big thanks to those who gave of their valuable time to read and comment on the manuscript of this book: Adina Zalesski, Angelea Panos, Ann Hearn Tobolowsky, Dawn Miller, Eric Evans, Heather Thorkelson, Kimberlee Calder Bryson, Lee-Anne Fox and Sarka Veronica. I am deeply grateful for your thoughtful and generous feedback. Thanks also to Katie Hafner, who read and commented on the early drafts of this manuscript. Finally, thank you to my wonderful online support team, who read and champion my work and send me messages of encouragement. Much gratitude to all.

ABOUT THE AUTHOR

Alda Sigmundsdóttir is a writer and sometime journalist. She was born in Iceland, raised in Canada, and has also lived in Germany, Cyprus and the United Kingdom. Alda has written extensively about Iceland for the international media and given talks and lectures widely about various aspects of Icelandic society. Catch up with Alda on her website aldasigmunds.com, where you can read excerpts from her other books and sign up for her newsletter. You will also find Alda on Facebook, Twitter and Instagram.

OTHER BOOKS BY ALDA SIGMUNDSDÓTTIR

The Little Book of Days in Iceland, an Illustrated Calendar

The Little Book of the Icelanders at Christmas

The Little Book of Tourists in Iceland

The Little Book of Icelandic

The Little Book of the Icelanders

The Little Book of the Icelanders in the Old Days
(available in English, French and German)

The Little Book of the Hidden People
(available in English, French and German)

Unraveled–a Novel About a Meltdown

Living Inside the Meltdown

ENDNOTES

M. Scott Peck, People of the Lie, the Hope for Healing Human Evil (New York: Touchstone Books, 1983) p. 42

www.ingramcontent.com/pod-product-compliance
Lightning Source LLC
Chambersburg PA
CBHW032151080426
42735CB00008B/669

* 9 7 8 1 9 7 0 1 2 5 1 8 4 *